History's Greatest Drinking Games

History's Greatest Drinking Games

From the notorious to the wisely forgotten

ELLIOT MARTYN

CONSTABLE

CONSTABLE

First published in Great Britain in 2025 by Constable

1 3 5 7 9 10 8 6 4 2

Copyright © Elliot Martyn, 2025
Illustrations by Emanuel Santos

The moral right of the author has been asserted.

All rights reserved.
No part of this publication may be reproduced, stored in a retrieval system, or transmitted, in any form, or by any means, without the prior permission in writing of the publisher, nor be otherwise circulated in any form of binding or cover other than that in which it is published and without a similar condition including this condition being imposed on the subsequent purchaser.

A CIP catalogue record for this book
is available from the British Library.

ISBN: 978-1-40872-309-8

Typeset in Adobe Garamond by Hewer Text UK Ltd, Edinburgh
Printed and bound in Great Britain by Clays Ltd, Elcograf S.p.A.

Papers used by Constable are from well-managed forests and other responsible sources.

Constable
An imprint of
Little, Brown Book Group
Carmelite House
50 Victoria Embankment
London EC4Y 0DZ

The authorised representative
in the EEA is
Hachette Ireland
8 Castlecourt Centre, Dublin 15,
D15 XTP3, Ireland
(email: info@hbgi.ie)

An Hachette UK Company
www.hachette.co.uk

www.littlebrown.co.uk

I am indebted to my agent, (not only) for her guidance and enthusiasm in this process; *iigaisu*.

To my parents and grandparents, for the innumerable history books you gave to me; here is one in return.

Finally, with deepest gratitude, to MTY for so very much beyond the bounds of these pages, but also for her support and wisdom on what is contained within them.

Contents

Author's Note ix

1. Flinging with Friends: Kottabos, Ancient
    Greece, circa 600–300 BCE   1

2. Beer, Ballads and Bemusement: Puzzle Jugs
    and Fuddling Cups in Early Modern
    England, 1500–1750 CE   9

3. Painful Pitchers: Pulque Bowls and
    Priestly Rituals in Pre-Colonial
    Central America, circa 700–1490 CE   19

4. Shooting for Shots: The Noble Art of
    Touhu in Ancient China and Korea,
    circa 500 CE–Present Day   29

5. Carnival Crazes, Gorzałka, Wódka and
    Social Lubrication: Drinking the
    Spirit of Poland, 1500–1935   41

6. With Friends Like These, Who Needs Enemies?
    Passatella in Italy, 1800 CE–Present Day   57

7. Scientific Sipping: Astronomy, Automata
    and Alcohol in Aristocratic
    Germany, 1400–1750 CE   71

8. History Rinsed with Vodka: (Un)diplomatic Drinking Games in Russia, 1200 CE–Present Day — 83

9. Bragging a Horn-full: Drinking Games and Viking-ing in Medieval Scandinavia, 750–1200 CE — 99

10. Something to Wash Down the Pearl? Drinking like an (Ancient) Egyptian, 3000 BCE–50 CE — 113

11. Drinking in America: Finding Booze in the New World and Under the Ban, 1600–1950 CE — 129

12. Highlands, High Duties, High Jinks: Scotland, Alcohol and the Union, circa 1600–1850 — 149

13. Libation and Liberation: Palm Wine and Akpeteshie in Ghana, circa 1850–1962 — 167

14. Jiuling and Fifty-Two Gifts: China's Amazing Array of Drinking Games and the Invention of Playing Cards, 4000 BCE–1911 CE — 181

Bibliography — 197

Author's Note

It is said that dogs are mankind's best friend, our constant companion and guiding presence. Indeed, padding gallantly across civilisations, evidence of our canine friends is there for all to see: a paw print in a Roman roof tile, a cave drawing of an almost-wolf; the glamorous existence of Marilyn Monroe's Maf or Soviet space dog Laika, testament to a (mostly willing) long-running partnership.

Yet there is another partnership with mankind, one cultivated across the globe and throughout history, taking a huge variety of forms, processes and flavours: the simple partnership of humans with sugars, water and untold trillions of benign microbial friends. Our partnership, of course, with alcohol.

Perhaps not always as beneficial as the dog, this badly behaved friend of the human race has followed us, unsteady on its feet, across history and culture. A drug compound used to relax, to indulge and to excite, a form of alcohol has been used by the majority of cultures across the world. Today it's the world's most popular and acceptable recreational drug, widely used and celebrated while also creating some considerable societal and personal health impacts when misused.

Yet despite – and sometimes because of – the misadventures it's led us on, alcohol has a rich story to tell about us as humans and the cultures that have shaped its development; about our rituals and celebrations, our economic and social relations, and our unquenchable thirst for fun. Indeed, and perhaps unsurprisingly, where alcohol has gone, games and rituals have practically always followed. From the Tang Dynasty to Soviet Russia, and from secret Highland whisky stills to the Maya temples of Central America, we've never run out of new, innovative and downright stupid ways to drink.

So, in the name of rigorous historical research, I've delved across time and space to compile a guide to history's most famous, notorious and bizarre drinking games, rituals and customs. It's a whistle-stop tour of the bold, bawdy and amusing habits of drinkers of the past, plus enough actual history to make sense of them and to justify requesting that your university library buys a copy.

And yes, there are instructions, but I can't say I'd advise following all (or perhaps any) of them. After all, trying to get a casual game of Kottabos going after a dinner party will ruin both your friendships and your carpet. Bottoms up!

Flinging with Friends

Kottabos, Ancient Greece, circa 600–300 BCE

The very next time you're invited to a symposium (an Ancient Greek drinking party), you can look forward to quite the evening of music, debate and poetry, all washed down with Greece's finest sediment-rich organic wine. Classical civilisation is synonymous today with sophistication, but, as you consider your sandal choices before heading out, you should also prepare yourself for the difficult, messy and sometimes romantically charged drinking game of Kottabos, and yes, you should probably bring a spare toga.

Ancient Greek civilisation spanned a period from 1200 BCE, following on from the earlier Mycenaean period, until 323 BCE, usually marked by the death of Alexander the

Great. At its glittering heights, around the fifth to third centuries BCE, Ancient Greece comprised a collection of over a thousand city-state territories spreading from Sicily across to modern-day Albania, Greece, the islands of the Ionian and the Aegean, to parts of North Africa and right across the western parts of modern-day Turkey. The most significant of these *polis*, or city states, included Athens and Sparta, as well as Syracuse, Argos, Rhodes, Elis and Corinth. They shared a common culture, language and series of grudges and were linked by trade, religion and diplomatic ties.

Greek city states were strongly militarised and independent, so wars between them were common. In fact, in 431 BCE, the drinking game of Kottabos was blamed as the cause of a major war between Athens and Sparta due to the kidnapping of Simaetha – sometimes referred to as a courtier and other times as an Ancient Greek slave – who was involved in the game.

Despite their bickering, the city states were highly organised societies with systems of government that protected their independence (and the power of local leaders). Systems were different from state to state but all had in common a form of male, aristocratic rule based on military survival; for example, the state of Sparta was ruled by two kings and an assembly of warriors. Athens, the most populous state, developed a sort of democratic(ish) system, where all male citizens (not all men were citizens) could vote on the leadership of the political system. Its large population and wealth supported the development of a booming artistic, literary and philosophical scene which became the model for much of what we think of as 'Ancient Greece' today.

In these militarised and male-dominated societies, sporting success was highly prized, and so too were male companionship and loyalty. In addition to battlefield exploits, men would compete for sporting prowess in competitions such as the original Olympics and socialise in the same close-knit groups of comrades and competitors. It was within groups and the wine- and music-filled parties they held, known as symposia, that men, and some women, would play the messy, drunken and sometimes scandalous game of Kottabos.

Sediment sports

As ancient drinking games go, Kottabos is one of the best recorded, with some serious classical endorsers – Pindar, Sophocles and Euripides all mention the game and its amorous allure. Pindar, for example, wrote of Kottabos and its links to love, noting how one dedicated one's 'turn' in the game to a member of the group one might have a romantic interest in: 'while getting drunk with Chimarus, I may toss the cottabus for Agathonidas.'[i]

At its most popular in the sixth and fifth centuries BCE, the game originated in Grecian Sicily before becoming fashionable across the Ancient Greek world, particularly in Athens, where it had become a trendy pastime for high society by 431 BCE. Kottabos was a serious endeavour and had become so well known that in its heartlands special circular buildings were constructed to play the game.

Kottabos was developed to make use of the particular qualities of Ancient Greece's most popular tipple, wine. Winemaking arrived in Greece (with grapes) during the Mycenaean era, having been first developed near modern-day Georgia around 6000 BCE. Greek wines were

---

i *Pindar, Fragments*, Loeb Classical Library.

categorised by region, with the finest stuff coming from the island of Chios and costing around two drachma (two days' wages for ordinary folk) for a *chous* (something close to three litres). Distinctions were also made between young wine, often for mass consumption by armies, and older wine, for the more discerning palate.

Ancient Greeks prided themselves on drinking their wine diluted, roughly one part wine to three parts water, with numerous ancient sources noting how this separated Greeks from the barbarous Macedonians, who dared to drink their vintages neat. In addition to its wateriness, Ancient Greek wine had another feature, which is central to the game of Kottabos: it was unfiltered and contained large amounts of sediment made up of yeasts, grape residue and other materials, which would settle at the bottom of wine cups known as *kylixes*.

The game focused on a single target, generally in the centre of a room, around which players arranged themselves. Each player would take their *kylix* (emptied of wine but with a residue of wine sediment still inside) and fling the sediment at the target using their right hand. Only the index finger could be in the hook of the cup and the other fingers had to be stretched out, palm flat. The player also had to be lying back on a couch, not unlike a chaise longue, and moved only their right forearm to launch the sediment at the intended target.

Kottabos Katakos (Kottabos with a pole) was the traditional and most commonly referenced variety. In this version the target of the game was a small bronze disc balanced atop a pole (the *plastinx*) in the style of a lampstand, with a larger disc (the *manes*) suspended halfway down the pole. A player would aim their sediment missile at said small disc. If they did so just right, the lumpen wine-residue would then fall with the dislodged target disc onto the larger bronze plate suspended below. This satisfying splat would create a bell-like sound, which was called a *latax*, the same name given to the residue itself, and which was the resounding marker of a successful launch.

Several other variations of the game existed, including Kottabos Oxybapha (Kottabos in a bowl), which was generally considered easier than the pole-mounted target. In this version a basin containing a number of floating saucers was placed in the centre of the group, and the object of the game would be to sink the saucers using the same sloppy projectiles. More unusual targets have also been found in Etruscan versions of the game (in pre-Roman Italy), perhaps the most innovative of which had the target as a bird statuette with a head in the shape of a penis, atop a tripod in a flat pan.

Players would fling their wine lees (another term for sediment) in rapid succession, so having the dexterity for a hit was cause for celebration and kudos, not least because success or failure in the game was often considered an omen of success or failure in love. Before a player flung their sediment, they would dedicate their turn, often to a lover or pal. The prizes that might be up for grabs were as varied in both value and ethics as eggs, slaves and romantic and risqué favours from other guests at the symposium. In one inscription on a vase, a Kottabos host exclaims, 'There are ticklings and the smack of kisses, there are the prizes I set up for the one who best shoots the Kottabos.'[ii] In

---

[ii] Brian A. Sparkes, 'Kottabos: An Athenian After-Dinner Game', *Archaeology*, vol. 13, no. 3 (1960), p. 207.

another depiction, a naked servant or sex worker holds in place the target disc, and a woman holding a *kylix*, poised to throw, declares, 'I am flinging this for you Leagros.' Similarly, the master Greek poet Cratinus once wrote of a *hetaira* (an Ancient Greek courtesan) dedicating her shot in honour of the tackle, so to speak, of Corinthian men.[iii]

The wine cups themselves were also part of the jovial and saucy fun of the party. Some believe players would bring their own *kylix* to Kottabos games, and some *kylixes* found in museums today include risqué pictures of scantily clad and rowdy symposia, while others have eyes drawn on the underside so as to continue a stare while the player drinks the dregs of their wine.

The popularity of Kottabos had waned by the time of Alexander the Great, and Roman sources were pretty snooty about the bawdy game of their classical predecessors. More modern re-enactments of wine sediment flinging in togas, such as the work of Dr Heather Sharpe, have demonstrated what a messy situation this game was, with wine lees likely splattered across all sides of the symposium and the players. Nonetheless, the wealth of surviving evidence around Kottabos allows us to understand the game in all its close, messy and sometimes steamy detail: as a bonding exercise for elite groups of aristocratic warrior men, and surely also as a way for them to avoid rinsing the dregs out of their *kylixes* before topping them up with yet more wine.

---

iii Brian A. Sparkes, 'Kottabos: An Athenian After-Dinner Game', p. 204.

How to Kottabos your *kylix* like a pro

Number of players: Unspecified, symposia were generally made up of male groups of elites, though evidence shows women were also active players of the game.

You will need:
- Unfiltered organic wine – several large urns' (or amphorae') worth.
- Water, to emulate the Grecian preference of drinking one part wine to three parts water. Or go undiluted, you barbaric Macedonians!
- *Kylixes* or wide-brimmed pedestal cups, preferably with risqué or jovial illustrations.
- A bronze saucer and plate affixed to a pole, floating saucers or a statue target.
- Several loungers or chaises longues arranged in a circle.
- A set of pre-agreed prizes or a group of open-minded participants.
- For advanced players, a special Kottabos room of circular proportions.
- Cleaning equipment.

How to play:
1. Players should be imbued with the spirit of the symposium before taking on the challenge of Kottabos. Food and wine should be first enjoyed, preferably with lyre music, poetry or some form of Grecian drama, before the Kottabos target is wheeled out.
2. In turn, each player sits back on their couch or lounger, taking an emptied *kylix* or cup with only wine lees or dregs remaining. They should hold it using only their

right index finger, palm facing upwards, ready to launch.
3. The player then dedicates a toast for their shot, generally to a lover or person of affection.
4. Using only their forearm, the player launches the dregs at the target in the centre of the room.
5. If the player hits the target and the *latax* falls satisfyingly onto the plate below, making a bell-like noise, then their chances of love or affection with the subject of their dedication are greatly enhanced and they then win a prize of the host's choosing. In a variation in which players shoot for forfeits and favours (something like truth or dare), individual players should agree terms before each shot. The author eschews any responsibility for such contracts and recommends playing for eggs or cakes, as some historical sources reference.
6. The game ends by mutual agreement and the distribution of prizes is equally a matter for general consensus. There are no records detailing who was responsible for cleaning wine stains from walls, togas and floors, but in all likelihood this would be a host's responsibility.

Top tip: the larger the clump of sediment, the more weight and control the flinger has over its direction and the more chance you have of knocking the target to the ground. And a final tip: choose your fellow symposians well and best make sure it's not your turn to host before suggesting a round.

Beer, Ballads and Bemusement

*Puzzle Jugs and Fuddling Cups in Early
Modern England, 1500–1750 CE*

The period from 1500 to 1750 was transformational for the British Isles, which – not for the last time – grew distant from Europe as the country broke abruptly from the Catholic Church over Henry VIII's marital divorce. In this period, too, the last English settlements in France fell, concluding a very messy few centuries of war, loss and plunder of our nearest but not that dearest neighbour. Britain was rocked by upheaval as King Charles I was beheaded and the monarchy deposed, plunging the country into a bloody civil war before the restoration of the crown. The Acts of Union in 1707 brought Great

Britain under a single monarch, while the crown continued to forcefully control Ireland and settle its northern province.

The twists and turns of this period also saw the rise and fall of the fortunes of many ordinary folk in the British Isles, with lives blighted by wars, poverty, religious persecution, disease and eye-watering taxes. As people migrated to growing cities, the pressure to feed a burgeoning urban population brought major changes to how food was produced, mechanising agriculture and leading to the development of early manufacturing, which would later become the Industrial Revolution.

While these shifts increased opportunities for some, the gap between the haves and the have-nots was growing. British merchants and traders grew wealthy on booming trade with new colonial possessions in the Americas and later India. These colonies, and the exploitation of them and their populations, fuelled economic growth and naval dominance for Britain, with new products like tobacco, sugar, tea, coffee, rum and spirits being sent to British shores from across the world to sell to groups of workers, merchants, and the emerging middle classes as they searched for new ways to spend their money and time.

As a result, Early Modern England, not wholly unlike its present-day counterpart, was a bawdy place where drinking was an ever-present part of life from the rich to poor. In the alehouses which sprung up across England in this period, barkeepers devised the most ingenious games, puzzles and drinking ballads for their patrons. It's often said (falsely) that this was a result of ale being safer to drink than water but the reality paints a more complex picture than one of cholera-preventing drunkenness. A growing associational culture, coupled with time and new income for more ordinary people, created new and hilarious ways to indulge, and pushed alcohol and the alehouse to the fore, to the celebration of some and the horror of others.

Ballads, wit and good company

For everyday folk, drinking was seen as part of a balance of natural 'humours', integral to a balanced lifestyle and to reaching socially celebrated attributes of wit and joviality, rather than simply as an escape from daily drudgery. Writing of the time transports the reader back to the heavy-drinking culture of alehouses, inns and taverns (think Falstaff, Hal and the merry folk of Eastcheap in Shakespeare's *Henry IV.I*), from ballads of drunken excess, boasting and tall tales to the pearl-clutching fears of those less prone to a tipple. Yet beyond these often delightfully bizarre texts, we are left with material evidence of some of the wackier means of consuming all this booze beyond the simple tankard or 'cup of sack'.

Historian Mark Hailwood, an expert on the drinking culture in Early Modern England, has helped define the link between associational culture and a growth in drinking places and drinking groups in this period. As part of his work he uncovered the example of a 1612 report by the constables of a Wiltshire town asking for help to stop a plague of alehouses, which stated: 'Doe all brewe and vie who maye brewe the strongest Ale and thither do resorte all the great drinkers bothe of the Towne and Countrie to spende theyer tyme in idleness and theyer monie in excessivie drinkinge.'[i]

In this particular case it was especially difficult to bring any of these idlers to justice as no one could be found to testify against the drunks; given that all those they questioned were drinking companions of the accused, a boozy omertà was unofficially held to keep the town in drink.

Much of the drinking boom in this period, where whole streets were seen to be 'but a continued Ale-house: not a shoppe to be seene betweene',[ii] was fuelled by a growth in income and leisure time, and with that came the formation of new types of social groups such as companies, friendly societies and more informal drinking bands. Within these roguish bands inebriation was a badge of honour, and literature celebrating it survives to this day. In 1628, writer William Prynne complains how drunkards are 'applauded' as 'Good-Fellows, wits Poets Courteous, Sociable, Merry, Jovial and boon companions'.[iii]

These drinkers enjoyed a self-affirming form of complementary writing to help their drink go down, in the form of the ballad. Printed on cheap paper, these ballads, affordable to much of the population, would be seen in alehouses, inns and taverns, and their tall tales and catchy verses would be sung by merry drinkers, perhaps egging on further drunken escapades.

---

i Mark Hailwood, '"Come Hear This Ditty": Seventeenth-Century Drinking Songs and Hearing the Past', *The Appendix*, vol. 1, no. 3 (2013).
ii Thomas Dekker, *English Villanies* (1632), quoted in Stella Achilleos, 'Puzzle Jugs in the Regency', *Regency Redingote*, 3 July 2009.
iii Phil Withington, 'Intoxicants and Society in Early Modern England', *The Historical Journal*, 54.3 (2011), 631–57.

One example written about by Hailwood is that of the 1630s ballad 'Roaring Dick of Dover, or the Jovial Good Fellow of Kent'. The ballad extols the virtues of good drinking; for Dick 'strong drink makes my wits quicker' and it suggests a competition among Dick's merry companions to 'drink, sing and freely pay'.[iv]

Many of these pamphlets, complete with woodcut prints of merry drinkers, survive to bring the bawdy bar-beating ballads home to us now. One verse that pulls no punches in its defence of drinking can be found in a popular pamphlet ballad titled 'The Claret-Drinkers Song' (introduced as 'Being a Pleasant New Song to the Times. Written by a Person of Quality'). It goes pretty far in seeing claret wine as perhaps the best thing known to earth:

> For all things in nature does live by good Drinking,
> And he's a dull Fool and not worthy my thinking,
> That does not prefer it before all the Treasure
> The Indies contain, or the Sea without measure:
> Tis the Life of Good-fellows, for without it they pine,
> When nought can revive um but Brimmers of Wine[v]

Puzzle jugs and fuddling cups

In the midst of all this merriment, mirth and misdeed, landlords were devising methods to keep their wayward

---

iv Mark Hailwood, '"It Puts Good Reason into Brains": Popular Understandings of the Effects of Alcohol in Seventeenth-Century England', in *Brewery History*, 150 (2013).

v 'The Claret Drinker's Song', English Broadside Ballad Archive.

flocks entertained in the pub for as long as possible. So behind the bar an increasing array of deliberately befuddling and bizarre drinking vessels could be found, the sole survivor of which, still in use in English pubs today, is the yard of ale. In the 1650s the most popular receptacle among these was the puzzle jug, a merry and messy method of quaffing (and spilling) large amounts of drink for the entertainment of your companions.

English broadside ballads

These wonderful ballads were far from focused solely on the virtues of drinking with one's boon companions. In fact, large collections of these early mass-consumed printed products survive today to give us a deep insight into the brilliant, the bawdy and the bad of balladry in all its glories. One open source digital collection, the English Broadside Ballads Archive, has nearly 10,000 ballads available for free online for you, dear reader, to peruse and no doubt sing uproariously at your leisure with your band of merry rogues.

The puzzle jug was designed to confound an already confused drinker on how best to consume its contents without spilling a drop. This complex crockery contained a series of interconnecting chambers, concealed lips, holes and pipes, ingeniously hidden using handles and decorations. Several holes in this network would need to be plugged with a drinker's fingertips in just the right way to avoid spilling the whole jug on their doublet.

BEER, BALLADS AND BEMUSEMENT

To increase the merriment, before the game began your charming and supportive companions would bet on your ability to solve the puzzle jug and drink the contents without mishap. One eighteenth-century jug from Liverpool reads:

> Here Gentlemen come try your skill
> I'll hold a wager if you will
> That you don't drink this liquor all
> Without you spill or let some fall.[vi]

Another puzzling pottery game used in much the same way in this period was the fuddling cup. These vexing vessels, popular in the seventeenth and eighteenth centuries, would've likely sat behind the bar or at the dining table ready to be picked up for light relief as guests tired of their companions' chatter or as the evening increasingly got rowdier to the tune of claret-y ballads. Not satisfied with just one bamboozling jug, the fuddling cup was a conjoined set of vessels, interconnected by a hidden series of pipes. Once liquid was poured in one cup, the jug could only be drunk without spillage if each cup was drunk from in the correct order.

Happily, many of these drinking artefacts and bawdy ballads survive, and puzzle jugs are a common sight in many local museums around Britain. Quite how readily you'd be able to borrow one for your own claret-fuelled bender is another matter.

---

vi 'Puzzle Jug', British, Liverpool, 30.70.3, Metropolitan Museum of Art.

How to puzzle jug, fuddle cup and drink like a witty English rogue

Number of players: A group of boon companions well versed in hearty drinking and with a full understanding of the benefits of alcohol to reach the lofty heights of wit, good-humour and joviality. These attributes should be much respected in your group.

You will need:
- Doublets, hats and supplies of snuff (don't actually do that) for the evening.
- Your finest puzzle jug and/or fuddling cups. If your local museum will not lend you a puzzle jug or fuddling cups, a couple of well-decorated plastic cups with some strategically pierced holes will do. For example, design a complex pattern and attach elaborate arms and appendages to the cup. Hide holes just next to where these appendages join the main cup or hide them within the natural complexity of your chosen pattern.

How to play:
1. Choose a local alehouse with a good reputation for strong drink and good food, and with ample supplies of ale, cider and claret.
2. Select a few choice ballads to extol the virtues of your chosen tipples, and which likely also lampoon the French and support the restored king for good measure. For inspiration, see the English Broadside Ballads Archive.
3. Once well availed of drink and hoarse with the merry singing of your favourite ballads, one of your number should bring out their finest puzzle jug and perhaps a set

of fuddling cups too to amuse you still further into the good night.
4. In turns your merry band will pour claret or a claret substitute of your choice into your non-watertight vessel, and before each attempt, your fellow drinkers will wager as to the chances of the drinker consuming all the claret without spillage.
5. The chosen drinker will have one chance to avail themselves of these perplexing vessels, needing to find the complex solution of drinking angle, finger grip and speed to prevent spilling the claret and losing their own, or their companions', bets.
6. Repeat with uproarious singing, drinking and merriment until the claret is dry or you reach the very height of witty good fellowship and agree to call it a night.

Painful Pitchers

Pulque Bowls and Priestly Rituals in Pre-Colonial Central America, circa 700–1490 CE

Meso-America is a term for the culture and civilisations which spread across modern-day Central America before the arrival of Europeans to the continent. This region flourished as a rich, complex and interconnected world before the brutal arrival of the Spanish and Portuguese conquistadors. This invasion sparked the end for the mighty civilisations of Meso-America, whose power was no match for the guns or the diseases brought to them by invaders.

Meso-America's huge variety of indigenous cultures can trace their origins back to early cultural groups, such as the Olmec people. The Maya, Zapotec and Totonac peoples grew out of these ancestral origins, creating their own cultural practices and building complex and well-designed cities, agricultural systems and monuments. While medieval Europe was dealing (badly) with the fall of classical civilisation (circa 400 CE) and generally having a pretty rotten time, over in Meso-America powerful and successful states were battling for dominance. It was only in 1428 that the most renowned Empire, the Aztecs, became the most powerful force in Central America, only to be defeated less than 100 years later by the Spanish conquistadors.

One consequence of the conquest of the Americas is known as the 'Columbian exchange', through which the wider world gained such new treasures as tomatoes, chilli, potatoes, tobacco and maize, along with gold and other wealth plundered from the empires of the region. In return, the indigenous peoples of the Americas caught and died in horrendous numbers from smallpox, measles and cholera, and those who survived came under the dominant rule of the Spanish and Portuguese, which would last until (and culturally beyond) the South American independence movement 300 years later.

This miserable 'exchange' saw the brutal repression of the Central American way of life, as cultural and religious practices were 'Europeanised' and the Catholic Church became the dominant religious force. However, some truly Meso-American practices endured quietly, even to this day, and were protected. One such cultural survivor is perhaps the oldest continually brewed beverage in the world, the humble drink of *pulque*, though some of its wilder drinking games and traditions are left to us only in record.

Pulque power

The tipple of choice in Pre-Columbian Central America (the time before the arrival of Europeans) was pulque, produced from the fermented sap of a giant cactus-like plant, which was consumed fresh and drunk with some surprising rules and rituals. Two thousand years later pulque is still drunk in Mexico today, in *pulqerias*. These traditional bars, often decorated with murals which Diego Rivera called the greatest examples of Mexican art, have successfully ridden out centuries of drinking trends and tastes and are once again enjoying a resurgence.

A white and sticky drink with an alcohol content somewhere between 4 and 8 per cent ABV, the enormous plants pulque is made from are known as the blue agave or the *maguey*, which can grow up to three metres wide, with spiked heavy leaves up to 1.5 metres long. In its biological function, the powerful sap is part of the plant's reproductive life cycle and, when not harvested for pulque, it fuels the plant's fruiting to shoot a giant stem eight metres into the air to flower, reproduce and then die, its noble work on earth complete. These giant agaves can take between twelve and twenty-five years to reach their spectacular final stage; there's no need to rush, evolutionarily speaking, when you're an enormous armoured cactus without any predators – at least until pulque was discovered.

When it's ready, a grower will cut out the 'heart' (or *meyóllotl*) of the early forming stem in the centre of the plant, a process known in the trade as castration. The grower then folds the thick leaves over to protect the then exposed hole, and this space is widened after a year. Into this pit runs the sweet liquid sap, which the plant is still creating to feed its now removed fruiting stem. This sap is collected and fermented naturally in wooden barrels where it turns to pulque in a few days. A good plant can produce sap in its open well for between six to twelve months before it dies. Pulque is a fresh drink and consumption naturally happens close to production; in rural Mexico today, *pulqerias* usually boast a white flag when a fresh shipment has arrived.

Gory gods

In classical Central America (among Maya, Aztec and other pre-conquest peoples) pulque had powerful links to godliness, sacrifice, power and status. With this complex mythology grew a host of rituals, rules and games to drink it, many of which are not recommended to try at home but we will provide instructions on how, *exactly*, not to try them.

The long timelines involved in pulque production are followed by an extremely short period of consumption – each cup is up to a quarter of a century in the making, then consumed fresh with almost no shelf life. The drink requires the necessary sacrifice of a giant maguey plant through the extraction of its 'heart', and this made pulque an unsurprisingly sacred and symbolic drink to many Meso-American cultures, including first the Maya and highland cultures of what is now Mexico and later the Aztecs, for whom it wasn't the only heart extraction process that went on.

For the Maya, pulque was closely linked to ritual sacrifice in what's seen by historian Lucia Henderson as a 'complex system of symbolic interchange between water, blood, and vomit, through which they alluded to deeper themes of purification, sacrifice, and renewal'.[i]

Maya pictographs showing the extraction of the fleshy 'heart' of the maguey plant for pulque production, and those showing the extraction of the fleshy heart of victims of religious human sacrifice – common in Maya and Aztec cultures – are remarkably similar. There are also drawings that show maguey thorns used alongside Gothic obsidian blades for use in bloodletting and sacrificial religious ceremonies. These gruesome links are part of a complex mythology found across Central America, where the origin of humankind was thought to be a result of godly self-sacrifice, and woven into this world of grizzly godly and human sacrifice is pulque and its parent, the maguey plant.

The clear connection between pulque and sacrifice doesn't end there: the Maya god of pulque was also the god of self-sacrifice. Pulque didn't just mirror grizzly ritual, though: for the Maya it was also a window out of the human world, albeit a more temporary one than their more bloody options. Pictographs show mortals drinking pulque among gods and in the underworld and it's inferred that Mayans viewed a nice boozy nap as a passage into the realm of the gods for a short period. In short, pulque's potency and stupor-inducing qualities appear to have enabled people enjoying a little shut-eye to briefly shuffle off their mortal coil and communicate directly with the gods.

Unlike the later Aztecs, Maya consumption of pulque was not just done through drinking. Surviving pictographs show the common use of enemas (reverse entry

---

[i] Lucia Henderson, 'Blood, Water, Vomit, and Wine', *Mesoamerican Voices*, 3 (2008), p. 54.

consumption, so to speak) in Maya drinking rituals. In addition to enemas there was also a practice of ritualised vomiting, potentially as a cleansing method. Though it's also possible this was just a side effect of trying to finish off a batch of pulque in one go, before it went sour. In research on indigenous pulque drinking among the modern-day Lacandon people in Central America, researchers found that *balche* (a similar drink to pulque) doesn't travel very well, so it's common for ritual ceremonies to involve drinking the entire stock in one sitting, which may suggest vomiting was less ritualised and more an occupational hazard.[ii]

Rabbits, drinking games and rituals

The Aztecs, too, linked the messy means of pulque-making with sacrifice and godliness, with several competing legends of gods discovering pulque. The Aztec gods of pulque were also the gods of warrior sacrifices, and before the festivals Ohtemalacatl and Panquetzaliztli the captive warriors about to be sacrificed were served one last dram of pulque.

Aztec culture was full of sage warnings of the danger of drinking and it appears that, despite Spanish colonial writing deliberately suggesting that the Aztec people were drunken and debauched, pulque was highly regulated and tightly controlled, with the drink generally reserved for those of high status and the elderly. Special vessels created for pulque ceremonies, including ones designed like maguey plants, have been found at grave sites for important figures, showing the significance and respect with which they treated the drink.

ii Lucia Henderson, 'Blood, Water, Vomit, and Wine', p. 61.

PAINFUL PITCHERS

Drunkenness in Aztec culture appears to have been seen as outright dangerous, but Aztec laws enabled priests, warriors, high-status and elderly people to drink pulque responsibly, while the rest might have the odd sample during special ceremonies. The wise warnings against drinking the fifth cup and abusing pulque's stupefying powers aimed to steer people away from dishonour, immorality and the less serious but still significant crimes of sleeping and becoming prone to singing.

The deity of Centzon Tōtōchtin, translated as 'the god of the 400 rabbits' (essentially a divine group of rabbits partial to debauched drinking parties), and the Aztec calendar day 2 Rabbit (1 in a 260-day calendar cycle) were very important in Aztec culture, with those born on the day of 2 Rabbit expected to be consigned to a life of drunkenness and vice. The date of 2 Rabbit and its relation to the movements of the moon was particularly important too for its pulque games and ceremonies. These included the game of *tochtecomatl*, which linked pulque and these divine rabbits to an unusual drinking game.

The main players of tochtecomatl were trainee priests to the Centzon Tōtōchtin (those 400 rabbits god of pulque). Apprentices of Centzon Tōtōchtin's drunken warren would dance in a temple plaza around a huge vat of pulque known appropriately as the rabbit jar. Within the jar were reeds to act as drinking straws, but there was an important twist: all apart from one reed contained holes above the pulque surface, making them useless to drink with.

The dancing would continue until a sudden cue, after which the young priests would dash in to grab a straw and suck at the great vat of boozy fermented plant sap. The lucky (or unlucky) young priest who had picked the one straw without holes had to drink the entire jar themselves, with the game repeating until the pulque stock was gone or the priests became totally comatose.

Another festival called Omeochtecomatl, the festival of the maguey scrapers, involved a similar game played not by young priests but instead by the pulque growers and fermenters themselves, drinking down decades of gentle plant rearing in one go. Today no such festivals survive, for better or worse, but pulque still holds a sense of great importance in the heartlands of modern Mexico. More recently, growers have at last developed a canning process which they hope will allow pulque to reach a greater number of drinkers and restore its place as the drink of Meso-American culture. It also means you can drink it a little bit less frantically than in a huddle of Aztec priests in training.

How to design your own pulque-based ritual night

Should you be able to get your hands on this highly perishable of commodity in the first place, many of the cultural practices which use pulque in this chapter are not really appropriate in the twenty-first century. Parties which involve the ritualised enema consumption and/or regurgitation of fermented cactus sap are likely to raise eyebrows, while the sacrifice of warriors deliberately intoxicated with fermented plant sap contravenes the laws of most countries.

However, within a limited field of options, you can re-create the festival games of the 400 rabbits with little to no legal or reputational risk.

PAINFUL PITCHERS

Number of players: Unspecified but many is good.

You will need:
- Pulque, either fresh or canned, in large quantities. You can use the information at the start of this chapter to make your own if you have the benefit of land and time (twelve years minimum), or else substitute in another low-ABV beverage in a pinch.
- A large ceremonial bowl, ideally featuring depictions of the moon and rabbits.
- A set of straws, all but one perforated above the pulque line in such a way as to render them useless for drinking. There should be one straw per player of the games.
- A large open space in which to dance uproariously to a set of vicious and sacrifice-demanding pulque-sozzled deities. You can borrow from Meso-American ones or make your own. We also have no idea of the music which would have accompanied these games so again this is open to your interpretation and no one can call you out on your choice!

How to play:
1. Players should assemble and agree on a set time and accompaniment to dance round the ceremonial bowl of pulque. An agreement should also be reached on the cue for the dancing to end.
2. The bowl should be filled with pulque (or your chosen equivalent) and the dancing should begin. At the agreed cue all players should rush to the bowl, taking a straw and beginning to suck at its end.
3. The player who has the one working straw will quickly become known and then the entire group should cheer on the player as they finish the entire bowl of pulque.

4. A new round can then begin and play should continue in this manner until the stocks of pulque or the players are exhausted.
5. Sacrifices are strictly not part of recommended play.

Shooting for Shots

The Noble Art of Touhu, Ancient China and Korea, circa 500 CE–Present Day

Drinking games are often associated with heady silliness, merriment and exuberance, but in ancient China and Korea the game of Touhu (in China), or Tohu (in Korea), translated as 'pitch pot', was a drinking game deeply rooted in earnest philosophical practice and played by the noblest of courtiers, princes, kings and eminent scholars. Touhu was a serious endeavour, one which proved one's worth before the noblest in the land; but even this courtly pastime had that silly human edge we find in all drinking games: the simple forfeit of a cup of wine for every failure or, failing that, the truly monstrous forfeit of singing a silly song before the court – think enforced karaoke alone in front of your biggest boss at work.

Touhu, in essence, was played between two courtly competitors who took turns as part of an elaborate ceremony to shoot special arrows into a specially designed pot. This was done either sitting or standing and prizes could be extravagant – a horse, for example – while the punishment was almost always to finish one's drink and upset the most desirable Confucian balance with a little too much of the good stuff.

As Chapter 14 will tell us, Touhu was far from the only drinking game played in ancient China, but it has a unique history in being shared in popularity in China and ancient Korea as well as a deep philosophical root in the teachings of Confucius. Touhu features in a range of ancient imperial paintings from Korean and Chinese courts, where archery was prized as a skill, and museums around the world still hold Touhu vases. Even today, particularly at Lunar New Year, and particularity in Korea, the game is played widely with simple game sets, available from major online retailers, not too different from those played in ancient times, though perhaps with slightly less of the serious Confucian rigour which its ancient rules demanded.

Confusing origins

Touhu originated in China, before spreading with Confucian thought to Korea, and it's likely TouHu was invented by idle soldiers throwing arrows into empty rice wine pots. Though the game's practice really has changed little since then, the conceptual world behind the game and its links to nobility, Confucian theory and personal rigour have moved on a lot from a bunch of war-weary archers taking it easy between battles.

The fact that Touho emerged during China's Warring States period as a drinking game based on the use of weapons and wine vessels is perhaps unsurprising: there was a lot of war going on and war mostly involves a lot of waiting around. From around 481 to 221 BCE the old supremacy of the Zhou dynasty, which ruled a league of cities across modern-day China, fell apart, challenged by a system of independent states and monarchs whose armies were in near-constant battle. This period was both terrible and influential, with conflict generating fresh philosophical theories and new political and strategic writers and institutions. The Warring States period ended in 221 BCE, when the Qin Empire's victory established the first unified Chinese state in history.

However, Touho's popularity wasn't drawn simply from it being good killing practice while drinking; in fact, this connection with the most noble skill of archery made Touho a pastime of kings and scholars and one which represented the most sacred tenets of Confucian thought. Archery was considered one of the Six Noble Arts of the Zhou dynasty, the values of which the Chinese thinker and semi-religious figure Confucius sought to transmit and popularise.

Confucianism is perhaps best described as a total way of living and being; somewhere between a religion, a philosophy and a practice, it has been the dominant ethical value system in East Asia for over two thousand years. It's not the case that contemporary Chinese or Koreans consider themselves Confucian, but as European thought on morality, selfhood and logic draws heavily from Europe's classical and enlightenment origins, so is the influence of Confucius felt in contemporary society in parts of East Asia.

Confucius, an archery teacher who lived in Lu (now near modern Shandong, China) from around 551 to 479 BCE, didn't invent new theories but revitalised older, ancient thoughts and practices common to the old Western Zhou dynasty in China, drawing on a real and imagined inheritance of an idealised and even more ancient China. Confucius sought to promote stability, rules of living for a good life and strong social bonds, which in a period of 'Warring States' seems sensible. These ideals and virtues are recorded as his form of resistance to the dominance of wealth and power in his contemporary Chinese society.

Confucian practice would spread rapidly through China and followed Han Chinese migrants as they travelled and settled abroad, where it emerged in Korea, and was closely linked, though distinct, to the introduction of Buddhism in Korea in 338 CE. Yet is was only after Buddhism's early emergence in Korea in the Goryeo dynasty that neo-Confucianism spread and with it the drinking game of Tohu.

The noble and ritualised skill of archery, and by extension the game of Touhu, was in Confucius's eyes (perhaps unsurprisingly given he was an archery teacher) one of the few ways one could engage in competition if one was to remain a dignified person, and the Zhou tradition included several ritual uses of archery from the 'three tier' rituals known as the li; a hunting ritual, a specific archery dance and the use of bows and arrows as part of the formal possessions of high office.[i] Behind its Confucian baggage,

i Stephen Selby, 'Chinese Archery', Asian Traditional Archery Research Network.

however, it remains clear that Touho was an acceptable way to have a jolly, inebriated time at court and drink wine with high society.

A most serious drinking game endeavour

The earliest codification of the rules of Touhu can be found the ancient *Book of Rites*, in which pitch pot is clearly considered a serious drinking game played at formal parties. In the rites, the pitch pot game begins with a protracted 'no no I couldn't' politeness battle between host and guest, when the host offers, 'I have here these crooked arrows, and this pot with its wry mouth; but we beg you to amuse yourself with them.' While the guest (somewhat sozzled) replies kindly, 'I have partaken, Sir, of your excellent drink and admirable viands; allow me to decline this further proposal for my pleasure.' This however doesn't stick, and the host replies, 'It is not worth the while for you to decline these poor arrows and pot; let me earnestly beg you to try them,' until eventually the guest acquiesces.[ii]

The rules as written in this most ancient of texts also seem to require the player to have a superintendent of archery who measures the distance between pot and thrower and a director of music and a group of *cithern* (an ancient Chinese instrument) players to play ceremonial music between throws. Thankfully the *Book of Rites* also helpfully sets out whether the host or the guest should bring members of the required retinue:

---

ii *Book of Rites* (Liji), trans. James Legge, *Chinese Notes*.

The superintendent of the archery, the overseer of the courtyard, and the capped officers who stood by, all belonged to the party of the guest. The musicians and the boys who acted as attendants, all belonged to the party of the host.[iii]

Glad that's cleared up.

In this version of the rules it's clear that Touhu is not a game for anyone but the highest in society. This probably isn't that surprising if the 'buy in' was several horses. The *Book of Rites* also calls for drink forfeits for the losers and horses (yes, horses) for the victors. The winner gave the vanquished a cup to drink; and when the cups of failure were dispatched, the superintendent presented the winnings to the victor, with the number of horses corresponding to the number of arrows (which must be made of mulberry wood) that landed in the pot.

The book also gives warning to players, with rules that seem to exclude too much frivolity in this most earnest of drinking games: 'Do not be rude; do not be haughty; do not stand awry; do not speak about irrelevant matters. Those who do any of these things must pay the penalty.'[iv] The penalty, of course, being to finish one's drink or drink another glass of wine and to sing a song in front of the assembled group. Horrifying.

The rules in the ancient *Book of Rites* were updated in 1071 (only a thousand years old so not ancient at all) by Sima Guang, whose new rules for the game more closely adhered to Confucian thought, toning down the already

iii *The Book of Rites* (Liji).
iv *The Book of Rites* (Liji).

quite limited frivolity and reorienting the game within a ritual framework.

Just as in ancient times virtue could be expressed through archery, so too could that virtue be expressed through pitch pot. In these rules luck and chance were more or less removed and in their place came a focus on how good, virtuous positioning, conduct and intellect was the key to winning Touhu:

> As one faces the pot and holds the arrow, in his nature there is no distinction between coarse and fine, there is nothing that is not sublime. Respect, attentiveness, and will power all rest in centrality and straightness. Though this state may not last long, one can use it to practise these qualities. Surely this is the way to order the mind.[v]

The writings of Sima also take out the 'luck' from the game. Describing the predetermination that someone without virtue simply cannot succeed in Touhuu:

> When the unworthy person plays this game, he bends his body, stretches out his arms, and uses tricks and artful devices. If he does not hit the target, he is not ashamed. Surely this is the way to recognise people's character![vi]

Evidence of the game can be found in the range of Touhuu pots in museums across the world, some with

---

v Philip Clart, 'The Concept of Ritual in the Thought of Sima Guang', in *Perceptions of Antiquity in Chinese Civilization*, Dieter Kuhn and Helga Stahl (eds) (Heidelberg: Forum Verlag, 2008), p. 246.
vi Philip Clart, 'The Concept of Ritual in the Thought of Sima Guang', p. 246.

complex scoring mechanisms like an extra eight additional cylinders to act as a target, and reliefs of Touhu are also found on stone tombs found in Nanyang, in southern China, evidently adorning the final resting place of some of the game's greatest ever fans.

Korean take-off

After conquering China, Tuho came to Korea through the Goryeo Royal Court, with King Yejong, a Confucian fanatic, recorded to have told courtiers in 1116, 'I would like to test the sophisticated Tuho instruments I received from the Sung Emperor,'[vii] and thus a hit was born. Under the various Korean dynasties that followed, Tuho was particularly popular with the royal courts as the rulers used Confucianism's resurgent popularity to promote their influence. The game gained notoriety and quickly spread from kings to courtiers and officials to scholars, not least as it was one of the few gaming pastimes where women could play with men. In fact, during wartime in medieval times women would build bows and arrows and use them to come to their city's defence by manning the walls as archers. Archery was an integral part of Korean society and continued to be seen as the high-minded game of Confucian rigour, but with some drinking forfeits and antics thrown in when played as Tohu.

Tuho crops up regularly in the annals of Korean royal houses from then on: it is used to placate visiting Chinese

vii Lee E-Wha, *Korea's Pastimes and Customs: A Social History*, trans. Ju-Hee Park (Paramus, NJ: Homa & Sekey Books, 2006), p. 83.

envoys, drunken bouts take place at King Myeongjong's fantastically titled 'Pavilion of Felicitous Gatherings', and in another example it gets the young crown prince off the hook for playing arrow throwing (and drinking) with the court eunuchs because Tuho was a 'respectable Confucian institution'.[viii]

In Korea Tohu still enjoys a central place in traditional celebrations, depicted on the 1,000-won note, and is commonly played at historical sites and more widely at home around Seollal (Lunar New Year) and Chuseok, a Korean autumn or harvest festival and public holiday. Now liberated from its exclusive past, Koreans can enjoy the game with less virtuous and complex rules and perhaps one or two cups of wine as a forfeit. Though even today the winners are called *hyeon* (wise) and the losers *bulseung* (no success).

How to play Touho with the upmost respect for Confucianism while having a glass

Number of players: Two at a time, accompanied by their courtly retinues, of course.

You will need:
- A set of fletched (feathered) mulberry wood arrows, square-shafted and rounded softly at the end. Modern Touho set arrows appear to be around 50–60 cm long.
- A Touho jar, either ceramic or metal, which in the *Book of Rites* has a diameter of 2.5 inches at the mouth, a neck of 7 inches and a belly of 5.

---

viii Lee E-What, *Korea's Pastimes and Customs*, p. 85.

- Red beans to fill the jar sufficiently to prevent the arrows from bouncing out or the jar from toppling.
- Wine, ideally Chinese rice or grain wine, but in extremis any wine should do.

For a courtly game of Confucian rigour, as specified in the *Book of Rites*, add:
- Several horses, to award to the winners.
- A director of music and a band of musicians to play courtly ancient Chinese music between each throw. The *Book of Rites* notes the piece 'The Foxes Head' as a worthy anthem for Touhu, though written music for this this does not survive so you may have to improvise this piece.
- A superintendent of archery to measure the required distance and bring the arrows to the players.
- Playing mats on which the players must kneel to make their throw.
- A counting stick to score with and counters.
- A game master.

How to play:

1. First, the formalities. The host must invite the guests to play; the guests must decline this offer twice. Only then can play begin.
2. Set the 'pot' between the players' mats, at a distance of 2.5 arrow shafts from each mat. For more than two players, ensure the jar is both central and equidistant from all the mats.
3. If the game is inside, there will be five rounds of four arrows each; if in a cloister or semi-open hall, seven rounds; and if in the courtyard, nine rounds.

4. In turn the players must throw arrows with the aim of them landing satisfyingly into the neck and body of the vessel. For the best results, do not forget to practise Confucian virtues (moderation, courtesy, care for parents, giving and close study) throughout this process.
5. The first arrow is worth ten points, the second and third five points each. The fourth arrow, known as *Yuijin*, is worth twenty points. One point is awarded if all but the first arrow go into the jar. No points are given for arrows not entering or entering backwards.
6. Once all arrows have been thrown, the game master will declare the victor and the other player/players kneel to drink their punishment wine.
7. This process then proceeds waywardly on with increasing drunkenness for a whopping nine rounds if played in a courtyard.

Top tip: bring your own mulberry wood arrows with a weight you're familiar with and be sure to check if the pot is weighted down or could be easily knocked. Practise your song.

Carnival Crazes, Gorzałka, Wódka and Social Lubrication

Drinking the Spirit of Poland, 1500–1935

Polish cuisine is world renowned for its warming and hearty classics – *pierogi* or *kluski* dumplings, rich stews, earthy soups – and for its fine meats and hundreds of speciality cheeses and local delicacies. To complement this rich fayre, Poland also boasts a dazzling array of traditional drinks, alcoholic and otherwise, which have quenched polish workers from hay harvests to factory finishes and much more in between. Poland lays claim to being the birthplace of *gorzałka*, a distinctly Polish vodka known as *wódka*, but also counts *kvass*, beer, apple wines, fruit liqueurs and spirits like

Slivovitz and Nalewki and non-alcoholic drinks like fermented sour milk, *zsiadłe mleko* or *podipiweki,* among its rich diversity of beverages.

Across its complex history, traditional drinks have flowed throughout Polish life, from the ubiquitous celebratory toast 'Na zdrowie!' ('to health') to their central role in ancient folk celebrations and religious rites. They accompanied weddings, funerals, harvests and hallowed days and marked the seasons in communities rooted closely (and at times forcibly) to the land and its produce. In among all of these functions, Polish drinks also lubricated a range of eye-opening games and drunken dalliances, some of which survive today and some we can only imagine. Yet there are hidden histories to Poland's drinking culture too. One such tale is the role of Jewish tavern keepers in the old Polish-Lithuanian Commonwealth (1569–1795 CE), who had a huge influence in distilling, selling and serving alcohol.

Napoleon reportedly encouraged his troops to be 'drunk as a Pole', not, as is often thought, a reference to Polish people being heavy or unruly drinkers but rather an admiration for the Polish style, in which one drinks well but keeps one's head. Across Polish drinking traditions we find unusual games, pastimes and traditions, from the spraying of fresh kvass, to the gorzałka-infused wedding and funerary rites, the inter-religious activities of the Jewish-run, serf-frequented tavern or the crazed carnival antics of Polish rural communities in the heady days before the arrival of Lent. In this chapter we explore Poland's unsteadier history.

CARNIVAL CRAZES, GORZAŁKA, WÓDKA

Poland's history in a glass

Poland's borders have had many versions (including some which did not exist at all), but Polish lands have over the ages broadly comprised the land running from the Baltic Sea across the steppe to the southern Tatra Mountains, with German-speaking and Czech-speaking territories to its west and the Kingdom of Rus', later Russia, to its east. Dominated by a great fertile swathe of land, food production, most commonly grain, would become the central occupation, resource and source of wealth for landowners, if not those who worked the land. Wódka, while today the undisputed king of Polish drinks, was not the first alcohol developed by the Slavic tribes which first settled what would become modern-day Poland. In these early groups, alcohol was often highly ritualised and central to almost any occasion, with missionaries to the region noting the common sight of a great ritual drinking vessel being passed around feasts to toast indigenous pre-Christian gods.

The formal Kingdom of Poland first emerged around 1025 CE; and some time from the later medieval period, following the introduction of stills from Western Asia via trade routes, it's likely that the first distilled spirits, the forerunners of Polish vodka, were developed. Distillation apparently arrived with much more civic-minded intentions, perhaps as a result of a small number of Polish physicians who studied abroad in Mediterranean cities where distillation techniques were being used in early medicine.

In 1569 the Polish Kingdom created a union with its northern neighbour to form the Polish-Lithuanian Commonwealth and became the largest state in Europe, running from the Baltic almost to the Black Sea. The

Commonwealth had a proto-democratic system of parliamentary rule and elected its monarchs, though voting privileges were only for nobles and serfdom remained the modus operandi of the economic system. For those wealthy few, and the merchant classes they patronised, this period can be seen as a 'golden age' where Polish architecture, culture and the arts flourished in a host of prosperous and modern cities.

The Commonwealth's position as a grain-producing superpower was due both to its fertile soils and hospitable climate and to the feudal serfdom structure of its rural economy. Much of its wealth from the medieval period onwards was the result of its ability to trade grain surpluses with the rest of Europe. Exports of grain peaked in 1618 at over 270,000 tonnes from Poland's main port of Gdansk; however, in 1648 a collapse of a trading system in the Baltic Sea and war with Sweden in northern Poland meant that the export of wheat was completely halted, leaving an enormous surplus of grain without a market.

In stumbles grain vodka, knocking older fruit spirits down the pecking order, the perfect use for the Commonwealth's surplus of grain. From the late sixteenth century, grain rather than fruit was used as a base for distillation and this was increasingly referred to as Polish wódka compared to gorzałka, which referred more often to other distilled alcohols, essentially fruit brandy or slivovitz. Wódka rapidly became a hit, with visitors to the Polish Commonwealth remarking on the frequency and vigour with which wódka was drunk by peasant and noble, man and woman alike. By the mid-eighteenth century, grain alcohol was making a third of all income of major estates in Poland.

All good things, however, come to an end, and by the late 1790s the Commonwealth's riches, its grain and population were seized upon in a series of partitions which divided the state into the control of its hungry neighbours in the Kingdom of Prussia, the Habsburg Monarchy and the Tsar's Russian Empire, wiping the state of Poland from the map of Europe for the next 120 or so years. Wódka, however, was not so simple to erase.

In this period of occupation, the ending of feudal ties to the land for peasants through the emancipation of serfdom, and industrialisation and growth in Polish cities, saw some major changes to Polish society. While little changed in terms of the difficult lot of rural agricultural workers and their predilection for wódka, rye grain began to face an upstart challenger to its wódka monopoly: the potato. By 1913 the overwhelming majority of spirits in Polish regions were potato-based, though 100 years later trends changed again and in 2009 only 3 per cent of spirits were potato-based, as producers returned to a more authentic 'grain-based' Polish wódka tradition.

'Christian' taverns and Jewish tavern keepers

Grain wódka was a fundamental of the Polish landowning class's income and hold on power. Their profit, from making and selling the drink on their estates, however, didn't end there, as serfs themselves were restricted to drinking only in taverns owned by their masters. Yet these taverns were intriguing for another reason, as they provided a meeting place for Jewish and Christian communities downtrodden by polish nobles and united by an unlikely mutual interest: alcohol.

> Serfdom was a feudal economic system of forced labour which developed across Europe but persisted in a more brutal form in Eastern Europe and Russia until the mid-nineteenth century. It fell out of use in Western Europe in part as a result of the Black Death, which gave greater powers and freedom to those peasants that survived its ravages and enabled them to force concessions from landowning classes.
>
> Serfdom had many localised varieties but in broad terms it essentially bound rural people to a specific landed estate with a portion of their labour and produce 'owned' by the landowner. Serfs would work for their landowner for a number of days per year, often at harvest or sowing times. In paltry return, they were given custody of a small parcel of land which they would work themselves, providing their lord with a tax on their produce which was sometimes paid in kind (often in wheat), the remaining portion of which they were allowed to keep for themselves.
>
> In Poland, a 'second serfdom' in the sixteenth and seventeenth centuries saw the practice tightened and enforced even more stringently to help grow the profitable export of wheat to Europe. The practice was formally eliminated in Russia and the lands it occupied, which included much of modern-day Poland at the time, in 1861.

For a long time, as historian Glenn Dynner's work has uncovered, Polish landowners had allowed the country's Jewish population, subject to an intense and deeply felt anti-Semitic suspicion and resentment, to occupy an economic niche in society: that of merchant for the sale of their goods and often the leasing and management of their businesses. In rural Poland, this most often meant the distillation, sale and service of alcohol.

The result of this complicated niche role and the unpleasant history of anti-Semitism, which gave few other economic opportunities, was that in Poland by the seventeenth century Jews were almost always involved in the running of the local village tavern leased to them by a landowner. This position, in the heart of rural communities, meant that Christian peasants and Jewish tavern keepers were constantly interacting, breaking bread and drinking wódka, admittedly in uneven class relations but ultimately both under the social and economic boot of their local nobility. In this mixer of cultures we find an intriguing coexistence where peasants relied on tavern keepers and tavern keepers relied on peasants, sometimes to escape legal persecution.

In Dynner's fascinating history of this phenomenon we see this in literary and numerical sources:

> It was Sunday, and from the church after morning mass,
> they came to ankel's to drink and relax
> In everyone's cup grey vodka swished
> 'round with a bottle the barmied rushed
> Yankel the tavern keeper, stood in the midst[i]

Indeed, in records of one Polish county between 1772 and 1779, 94 per cent of taverns were Jewish run and the

---

i Adam Mickiewicz, *Pan Tadeusz* (1834), quoted in Glenn Dynne, *Yankel's Tavern: Jews, Liquor, and Life in the Kingdom of Poland* (New York: Oxford University Press, 2005), p. 14.

other 6 per cent tended to have less Christian- and more Jewish-sounding names.[ii]

The Polish tavern operated at the centre of the village, a place to drink, eat, stay and wait out the weather, to borrow or save money, and to buy foods and goods; with the money serfs spent ultimately returning to their landowner as the owner of the tavern. Some sources visiting taverns in the Polish-Lithuanian Commonwealth reported on the Jewish tavern often with the bile and hatred of historically widespread anti-Semitism, degrading them as altars of devil worship, uncleanliness and bizarre customs. Tavern keepers were frequently chastised and even assaulted for their prices, with one particularly vile Polish proverb declaring 'the peasant drinks at the inn and the Jew does him in', yet Jews themselves were forced to pay exorbitant fees for the right to distil and sell wódka at all, a taxation and regulation that would eventually expunge their right to run taverns entirely.

Less orthodox sources show that these taverns were really hubs where members of the two faiths rubbed along together bound by their place in a deeply unfair, authoritarian and anti-Semitic society. Dynner finds that Jewish taverns became a central part of Polish-Christian folk customs and events, with Jewish musicians accompanying events and mixed communities dancing and singing to Slavic and Yiddish songs and wild drinking customs. Later on, as Jews were increasingly legally persecuted to remove them from their place in the economy, Christians would take a role in fronting their businesses to prevent them from being discovered running a tavern. Some sources too give us an insight into taverns as a place where genuine, if sometimes tense,

---

ii Glenn Dynner, *Yankel's Tavern*, p. 16.

religious debate could take place, with reputations for good conversation, good wódka and good borscht.

For Jews, too, the Jewish-run tavern was of great importance and, far from their sober reputation, one which they could enjoy to the full. For travelling Jewish merchants, often selling raw materials on behalf of landowners and producers, the tavern was a homely and safe place to stay on often hostile roads. For the Jewish Hasidic movement the tavern was a place to acquire alcohol central to their appreciation of the divine. For this strand of Judaism, which became popular in Eastern Europe in the eighteenth century, joy of worship, at the time enhanced by the drinking of alcohol, usually spirits, was a key tenet of belief. Contemporary depictions of Hasidic Jews in the period typically have them holding a bottle of wódka, while Hasidic songs from this time show clearly the role of alcohol in their religious practice:

> let us all together together/ greet the rebbe . . . let's all
> drink wine and pour the whiskey down our gullets/ raise a
> rumpus till the break of day[iii]

All this brewing, tavern keeping and drinking by Jews, Hasidic and otherwise, however, did not escape the gaze of the more moralistic of their community, and at this time large numbers of polemics by concerned rabbis can also show us how deeply linked tavern keeping and drinking were in the Polish-Jewish community. Rabbis wrote with grave concern about Jewish tavern keepers employing gentiles (non-Jewish people) to keep the tavern on the sabbath, or

---

iii Glenn Dynner, *Yankel's Tavern*, p. 40.

raising pigs as they could be fed the waste product from wódka production, or simply for drinking too much, too outrageously or too publicly.[iv]

A bounty of Polish country drinks

Before wódka, the first spirits in Poland were drawn from fruit ferments distilled usually from plums to around 70 per cent ABV and known as Slivovitz. Most popular in the south of the country, this powerful spirit, which is a close cousin of Balkan raki, is still produced, often illicitly. Other fruit liqueurs, known as *nalewki*, are also popular and ancient Polish drinks, made using sour cherries, blackberries and wild apples and fermented for two years to produce a roughly 45 per cent proof country-style fruit spirit.

Kvass, a Slavic speciality found across Eastern Europe, made by fermenting bread, is an ancient drink consumed in the hot summers of Poland, Russia, Belarus and Ukraine. A light golden brown low-alcohol drink, it was commonly produced at great volume for the grain harvest while stronger versions were commonly prepared for festivals and feast days. Kvass was simply produced and had a variety of recipes but was usually made by soaking old, dry bread (ground down) in warm water and allowing it to cool.

Another popular folk drink associated with working the land, apple wines were produced across rural Poland (traditionally apple trees were planted along roads and most households would be able to find wild apples to produce

---

iv Glenn Dynner, *Yankel's Tavern*, p. 65–66.

apple wines or strong ciders). Beer, traditionally millet beer and mead, were also Polish staples in the medieval period.

Wódka, both rye and potato, is Poland's famous modern beverage and we've already covered its development from medical uses to grain surpluses and the sale of rye wódka back to the peasants that produced it by Jewish tavern keepers and producers. The arrival of the potato as a crop from the New World lowered costs further and propelled potato wódka to become the drink of a newly freed peasant class no longer tied to the land of their birth. By 1920, wódka duties were funding much of Poland's resistance to Soviet expansion and in 1925 the state monopolised wódka production entirely. From then until 1989 production was centralised, industrialised and removed from the rural and artisanal roots which had developed rye and potato vodkas. Poland had once boasted 900 or so distilleries but by 2017 only eighty-four remained.

In recent years, however, a resurgence of demand and pride in distinctly polish rye vodka, and a reputation for quality, has rejuvenated the flagging industry. Today Polish law decrees that true polish wódka must be 97 per cent grain spirits, and rye is prized for the bitter and fragrant nature of its taste, which distinguishes Polish wódka, designed to have bite and character, from Russian vodka, which often prides itself on the most smooth and very subtle flavour.

Drinking games and folk drinking traditions

With such a range of traditional drinks, Poland unsurprisingly has a wonderful history of consuming them in the wackiest of ways. Poland's folk traditions run deep, with feast days in almost every month, a rich tapestry of foretelling and foreboding omens, and sets of rites and rituals for every stage of life, from cradle to grave. In many of these traditions we find an intertwining of celebration and the traditional drinks, carefully prepared by those with little, which accompanied these precious moments of levity in otherwise hard and humble lives on the land. From exploding kvass battles to wild weddings, tavern antics or the peculiar folk traditions in the heady carnival days before Lent, these wacky and equipment-heavy drinking games and customs will keep you occupied for some time.

Volcano kvass

In the heartlands of traditional Polish kvass country, in a village known as Zaława, the fine spring waters and home-baked bread produce the Moët of Polish kvass, recognised by the Polish government for its exceptional quality. Traditionally in this region, a strong kvass is prepared for feast and festival days, and during those exuberant celebrations the residents of Zaława are renowned for holding a veritable street battle with the highly carbonated kvass it is so well known for. This game, known as volcano, involves simply shaking a bottle of fine kvass to its very limit and releasing the force of its powerful fermentation in the direction of an unfortunate target. Another method includes the shaking of a bottle in secret before 'giving' a nice refreshing kvass to an unsuspecting victim who proceeds to open the enlivened bottle only to be covered in the lively, bready, yeasty liquid before they know what's taken place.

Tavern antics

A most unusual drinking game could be found in the local tavern in the days before Lent, when taverns were usually presided over by Jewish leasers who distilled and sold vodka to the local Christian peasantry on behalf of their mutual landowner, the local aristocrat. In these melting pots of Jewish and Christian tradition, Jewish music accompanied shared folk traditions including the preparations for Lent. In some records, Jewish tavern keepers took part in festivities by setting up a log in the centre of the tavern; older women would then tie younger married women to the log in a (one hopes good-natured) ransom until they or their husband paid a bounty of a bottle of vodka. This old-age attack didn't stop there, however, as the elderly would go from door to door demanding eggs to exchange for vodka at the tavern while in the fields workers were driven to the tavern in droves to join the celebrations which were accompanied by dancing and singing.[v]

Zapusty or carnival days

The days before lent, known as Zapusty or Carnival Days, went further still in rural communities. While today Shrove Tuesday (aka Pancake Day) is a nod to the using up of luxuries before Lent's privations, in rural Poland they really took this principle several levels up. A highly anticipated part of these annual festivities was the custom of sleigh parties, where sleighs designed in outlandish forms as bears, birds, bulls or other

---

v Glenn Dynner, *Yankel's Tavern*, p. 29.

impressive incarnations were prepared and parties of merrymakers would ride unannounced to the homes and farms of their unsuspecting neighbours accompanied by musicians. Upon arrival it was the custom to invite in the merrymakers and give them food and drink, after which a great party would ensue with folk dancing, games, sometimes hunting trips and the drinking dry of the household in question. When supplies ran out it was traditional for the hosts to join the sleigh procession and continue on to the next unsuspecting neighbour to dance and drink their fill again before the privations of Lent began.

Another boozy custom of the Zapusty, somewhere between a game and a ransom (are not all the best games so?), was found in Krakow and known as *babski comber*. In the last few days before Lent, the streets of the town were increasingly filled with outlandishly dressed flower vendors and other tradeswomen, each of them dragging a carefully made straw figure known as a *combra*. It was tradition that any man who crossed their path was quickly taken hold of and forced to dance with them, and presumably their *combra*, until they bought their escape with a round of drinks for the women. The festivities ended with the deliberate destruction of all the straw figures in the centre of the town, though no doubt not before many a man had left the city's streets for fear of further encounters.

Weddings and wakes

Wódka too was central to weddings and wakes in Polish tradition. Any suitor was expected to bring a bottle of wódka when he went to request the hand of his beloved.

The bottle should have a red ribbon and the young man's chances of success were communicated through a delicate drink-based action. The prospective bride was asked to go and fetch a glass, but if she went to the next room and failed to return, it signalled the refusal of the family to countenance the marriage; if she returned quickly with a glass, it was a sign of good prospects and if another glass was proffered then the marriage discussions could go ahead, but not before all had raised a glass and tried the quality of the suitor's wódka.

At wakes, too, wódka played a central role in the sometimes boisterous night watch that families and friends would perform over the deceased. Wódka, bread and coffee were proffered to sustain the long night and it was often that these wakes became raucous affairs, brushing the deceased lips with wódka as a nod to involve them in the festivities being held in their memory.

From Lent to life's end, harvest to marriage, drinking games using Poland's bounty of traditional tipples offer a fascinating glimpse into the life of Poles past. While few of the games described above are played in this way today, Poland still has a strong and proud attachment to its folk culture and its popular history, evident from traditionally celebrated religious festivals to its produce and much favoured national drinks. Na zdrowie!

How to celebrate carnival season with the zeal of a rural Polish village

Number of players: It takes a village.

You will need:
- A sleigh or other climate-applicable mode of transport, perhaps a go-cart, wheeled soap box or other non-mechanised and decoratable wheeled or sledded vehicle.
- A good stock of Polish wódka, fruit brandy or liqueurs, ciders, beers or, if you can find it, kvass. Ideally a range of drinks and a good table of Polish delicacies would be on offer.

How to hold a proper Zapusty:
1. Agree roles within the group. In the modern era, the surprise arrival of revellers atop decorated sleighs demanding the entirety of a household's food and wine has a wholly different social connotation. Some people should be designated to be descended upon and ideally some support to stock their larder might be given by the rest of the group.
2. Decorate the carnival vehicles, using traditional Polish folk colours and designs to bring brightness and beauty to your spring-bringing sleighs.
3. Spring the 'surprise', bringing music, dancing and drinking games to your gracious and hopefully forewarned hosts. Consider finding some traditional folk dances to learn and prepare a good Polish spread for the table.
4. Once feasted, move on to the next house, but please do warn them before.

Top tip: Zapusty was often planned months in advance in the long winter months so consider preparing the sleigh well ahead of time for maximum impact.

With Friends Like These, Who Needs Enemies?

Passatella in Italy, 1800 CE –Present Day

Italy is a country where tradition and obligation run deep, where family and community are bonds that hold firm, redoubled over time and reflected in culture, and in games. In the originally Roman drinking game of Passatella, these traditions, obligations and expectations mix with alcohol and power to create a cruel-spirited drinking game which will almost always end in tears and, just occasionally, in blood.

Passatella's ancient, if not venerable, origins in ancient Rome tell us little of how it was played but records suggest its infamous reputation preceded it even then. Horace wrote scathingly of the game 'King of the Feast', which is likely to have been Passatella,[i] while Cato seeks to avoid the game's messy fallout by asking, when among his friends, that Passatella games 'not be allowed to begin; it is enough to be your neighbour'.[ii]

Cato was perhaps wise in his advice, given Passatella was then and continued to be a complex game of intricate social reading, wit and oratory; and duplicity. The aim of the game was to monopolise one's share of a central 'pot' of drink at the expense of one's peers through weaving a web of obligations, debts and exchange. Pairs of players each take a turn at being 'masters', who can distribute the drink to certain players and exclude others subject to negotiation with the other master. In this simple format the most complex, sometimes decades-long feuds and campaigns can take place all for just a glass more than your neighbour.

As the game evolved, so grew its reputation, surviving the Roman Empire's demise and fragmenting into regional versions as the different regional polities of the Italian peninsula broke up into city states. This variation in styles of the game persisted in the game's later versions, both in urban Rome where it gained an infamous reputation for brawls and bloodletting in the nineteenth century and in rural southern Italy where it was often played by farm labourers.

---

i Émile Haguenin, 'Un Poète Romain: Belli', *Revue des Deux Mondes* (1829–1971), *CINQUIÈME PÉRIODE*, vol. 8, no. 3 (1 April 1902), p. 674.

ii Marcus Porcius Cato, *On Agriculture (De Agri Cultura)*, trans. W. D. Hooper and H. B. Ash, Loeb Classical Library no. 283 (Cambridge, MA: Harvard University Press, 1934), p. 56.

Decried as a drinking game of 'rare stupidity' which 'dates back to the ancients',[iii] one late nineteenth-century account from Rome made two wonderfully melodramatic comments on the game, the first that it was the game to which 'the primacy of knives' belong, and the second: 'Without wine, there is no Passatella.'[iv] Passatella is still played today, though one hopes with fewer actual casualties, even if friendships are lost along the way.

The origin of the origin of many bar fights

More recent references to Passatella come from nineteenth-century Rome, where European aristocrats essentially on fancy gap years (termed 'The Grand Tour') used it to colourfully illustrate their accounts of the spoiled grandeur and roguish danger they encountered on the Italian peninsula. We find later accounts from twentieth-century Sicily where anthropologists, somewhat condescendingly, were fascinated by the game as a window into what they saw as southern Italian 'peasant' life.

Rome of the early nineteenth century was a society reeling from a rude awakening, after the unbroken millennium-long rule of the Pope over the Papal States and neighbouring provinces was shattered by Napoleon's capture of the city in 1798 and his exile of the Pope. French soldiers briefly established the 'Republic of Rome' but this was to last only a year, after which the French were ignominiously expelled

---

iii Émile Haguenin, 'Un Poète Romain: Belli', p. 674.
iv Anonymous, *La Passatella: Spubbricate in Itajano e in Romanesco* (Rome: Edoardo Perino, 1889), pp. 56–7.

by the Austro-Russian liberation of the Italian peninsula in 1799, only for Napoleon to recapture Italy *again* in 1800, this time allowing the Pope to keep Rome and his states. This balance was undone once more in 1809 when Napoleon re-annexed Rome, only for the eternally exhausted city to be restored to the absolute control of the Pope in 1815 at the Congress of Vienna.

As stirrings of a new Italian nationalism that would come to unite the peninsula in the 1870s began to emerge, a phenomenon was also increasingly seen in Rome in this unsettled period, that of the 'Grand Tour-ist'. From the seventeenth century, wealthy, aristocratic Europeans could be found, bewildered on the roads, among the ruins and in the resplendent cities of southern Europe in pursuit of the classical ideal. What tourists like Christopher Wren in the 1660s, or later tourists like Lord Bryon or Oscar Wilde, sought was a simple idealised vision of classical civilisation, their recounting of which would reshape northern Europe's architecture, education and culture. This fuelled the Romantic movement's yearning for a pre-industrial Eden and the neoclassical desire to build a new Rome, grander even than seen on their travels, as a 'fitting' capital for each of the expanding and bloody European empires.

Italy at this time was not an easy place to travel, with an array of city states and regions, each distinct in dialect, currency, custom and cuisine. A reputation for danger, roguishness and impropriety was seized upon happily by Grand Tourists, and they amplified this slightly xenophobic image of travel in the Italian peninsula as a daring venture, to reclaim the inheritance of classical civilisation from brigands, ruffians, bloated Popes, feudal customs and elegant disorder. This image persists in the histories of late Papal

Rome which recount 'days of artists, foreigners, beggars, bad drainage, fevers, continual festivals, picturesque if somewhat senescent [antiquated] customs, loose morals'.[v]

The most argumentative of games

Passatella's reputation lent itself perfectly to these types of narrative accounts of Rome's rakish decline by Grand Tourists from Britain, France and elsewhere as a game designed entirely to provoke fights, often ending in blood – essentially the Monopoly of its time. One 1889 writer warned of the game's conclusion that if 'there are no good souls ready to intercede, from words it comes to blows, until a blade flashes that sends one to hospital and the other to prison'.[vi] Another traveller's diary in the early nineteenth century recorded two deaths in a single day as a result of two different games of Passatella.[vii]

The game's violent repercussions in society had long been a fear among authorities, who banned it. Pope Sixtus V (1585–1590) was rumoured to have tried playing it with his aides despite his own ban, but he himself is said to have grown so frustrated as his aides refused him drink within the game that other clerics intervened to prevent violent scuffles breaking out. Suffice to say, this author could not

---

v William Roscoe Thayer, review of *The Last Days of Papal Rome, 1850–1870* by Raffaele De Cesare, Helen Zimmern and G. M. Trevelyan, *The American Historical Review*, vol. 15, no. 2 (January 1910), p. 389.

vi Anonymous, *La Passatella*, p. 58.

vii Susan Vandiver Nicassio, *Imperial City: Rome under Napoleon* (Chicago: University of Chicago Press, 2005), p. 35.

find any definitive sources which indicate this rumour to be true, but it's a pleasant little distraction. Nonetheless, the ban, which was very real, remained in place as late as the early twentieth century, with Hargreaves's 1930 *Encyclopedia of Card Games* entry for the game warning would-be players that they would be responsible for 'any fights arising from the game as rissa (riot)'.[viii] This ban didn't seem to be very successful, however, as a French visitor to the city, Edmond About, in 1861 remarked rather wonderfully that, 'It is a forbidden game, but in Rome nothing is allowed and everything is done'.[ix]

Passatella as a game functions only through the relations, obligations and social power structures of the group that plays it over and over again, developing a micro-society, a mirror of social structures in the world outside the tavern. Passatella's gameplay relies on the deliberate exclusion and defamation of one or more players within the group who are made 'ormo' or 'ulmo', with ormo deriving from the word for elm. This insult, which in modern translation has lost some of its punch, roughly equates elm with being a weak and dry wood used in the production of wine but indirectly, merely to hold up the vine, producing no fruit or merit on its own. No doubt this joke was a cracker in the ancient vintner community and really caught on, despite it now being translated as 'you are like a stave of weak elm wood used to prop up the grape vines, secondary and inessential to the production of both fruit and wine and no good for furniture making either'.

viii J. Davies, 'Passatella: An Economic Game', *The British Journal of Sociology*, vol. 15, No. 3 (Sep., 1964), p. 194, quoting *Hargreaves, Encyclopedia of Card Games* (1930).
ix Edmond About, *Rome of To-Day* (1880), p. 81.

To be made ormo by the game's 'masters' was to have your game, evening, sometimes life, made a misery. With each turn the masters would use their power to grant other players the right to drink or to exclude them from drinking entirely, a bold move considering everyone playing chipped in for the drink at the game's centre. To be excluded by the masters in the game's older forms was also accompanied by a torrent of abuse, disguised as the rationale for why the ormo was excluded, passive as the elm stakes holding vines up in the fields. Exclusion, though, was often accompanied by humiliation, with an expletive rant as a rationale as to why they had been excluded. One recorder of the game noted an example: 'Giuseppe doesn't deserve a drink since his wife is sleeping with X'.[x]

Dear reader, you will no doubt be thinking, Why then do these people play? To play so the group can mock one of their number so virulently and defame their friends, their families and generally risk having your name dragged through the mud. The answer is predictably human: to be a part of it all and crucially to get one over on your rivals, friends, family and community. It is clear that these relations, the strength of bonds, obligation and interrelation of tight-knit communities up and down the Italian peninsula underpinned the unwritten 'rules' of the game which made it so popular. It was, in essence, a game of maintaining and obtaining honour and dealing out, while avoiding humiliation, as well as drinking as much as possible.

The other more contemporary source for Passatella, in

---

x Russell L. Langworthy, 'The Peasant World View: Italy and India', *Human Organization*, vol. 27, no. 3 (Fall 1968), p. 216.

English at least, crops up in a different Italy again: twentieth-century rural Sicily. Passatella is a regular feature of southern Italian scenes in classic cinema, such as *The Law/ Le Loi* (Dassin, 1959), where a rich northern Italian confronts the dark and rigid hierarchies of a southern Italian, Passatella-playing village he visits.

Far from the grandeur and allure of Rome, sources show the widespread popularity of Passatella in rural southern Italy, particularly among agricultural workers. Even as late as the 1960s, agricultural organisation and rural customs had changed little in a Sicilian economy that provided not much more than subsistence for those working the land. In these villages and towns, playing Passatella enforced, mirrored and sometimes mocked the strong social hierarchies that the south, particularly Sicily, was notorious for. Playing Passatella was an escape of sorts but one that at all times aimed to maintain honour, which was likened by one sociologist to being 'like money in the bank'.[xi]

The highly dedicated anthropologist J. Davies recounts Passatella being played in Sicily in most detail, having spent two and a half months playing it in one wine shop in a rural Lucanian town called Bolgiaquintan every night. His account speaks of the inherent unfairness of the game and the layers of imbedded relations among people who played together week in, week out for decades: 'Ideally, as I found by experience, there is no altruism in the game, no "fairness", no question of giving a drink because a player has been ulmo for the whole evening,' and, 'It is always a gain in prestige to gain a permanent advantage over a

---

xi Russell L. Langworthy, 'The Peasant World View', p. 216.

friend by breaking the relationship and failing to return a favour.'[xii]

Playing Passatella

The actual playing of Passatella is straightforward in terms of rules: two players are decided via lots or cards to each be the master, boss or *padrone*. The players collectively buy a portion of drink and prepare enough glasses for only some of the players, perhaps four out of six assembled. Each master then proposes to the others who of the group should receive their cup, and it is this action of giving drink to other players that amasses reciprocity and relations over time, for in Passatella players do not forget good or bad deeds done to them.

> It appears the Roman version of the game may have been played with dice rather than the cards of the contemporary version, to establish the game's hierarchy of 'master' and 'ulmo' or *padrone* and *sotto-padrone*, who drive the inequality of the game that provides its spice.

Thus if a player you consider in your game family is not a *padrone*, you might propose they drink. In addition, if you as a *padrone* find yourself with fewer allies around the table you might offer a drink to a game rival in order to foster returns for yourself and maintain a good portion of

[xii] J. Davies, 'Passatella: An Economic Game', *The British Journal of Sociology*, vol. 15, no. 3

the drink through denying others. Equally, against some players you would immediately deny them drink if they have done the same to you to keep the relationship dry and maintain your enmity.

It is for the other *padrone* to, usually, reject your proposals and sometimes even debate the order of which master makes the first proposal of who drinks. From there ensues a complex and ever-escalating debate of wit and complexities as roughshod and bawdy declarations are made of why a player should or should not drink. This friction and debate is vital for the game and *padrones* will often resign their position if they are partnered with a *padrone* who will agree with them. A standoff between masters sees an ever more complex and intense escalation of negotiations about who to invite to drink – with various strategies made until eventually all combinations are tried as they attempt to repay, exchange or create drink debts in their favour and maximise the flow of drink to themselves through the course of the games that evening, week, year and decade. Once all strategies are exhausted the entire affair degrades into essentially a modern-day roast battle.

These highly formalised rules, however, are also invitations to break them, for another prized element in the game is that of *furbo*,[xiii] to be cunning or skilful or, in practice, to cheat. To make a bargain or promise to a game friend but then outwit him adds to the layering of debt, vendetta, obligation and donation within the game and increases the prestige of the player. Davies notes the example of game friends Sarmiglione and Alichino: the former bargained with the latter to promise a finger of beer between whichever of them was ulmo that round, as an insurance offer. But while the

---

[xiii] J. Davies, 'Passatella: An Economic Game', p. 195.

'finger' agreed was a vertical depth, the finger eventually given to Alichino, who was unlucky enough to be ulmo, was the horizontal measure of a finger. He objected and so Sarmiglione declared the bargain abandoned and gave him nothing at all, drinking the whole glass himself.[xiv] More often than not such agreements in the game are made not to engender sharing but to create opportunities to exploit one's friends, leading to endless quarrelling – which some might see as the object, rules and outcome of the entire game.

The actual definition of 'winning' Passatella is slightly murky and in some cases the winner of the game may not be the winner in terms of honour. For example, in one account a writer notes that, 'Giuseppe was generally considered the real winner although he was ulmo and lost by the overt rules. He really won because he did not lose his dignity under extreme provocation.'[xv]

We can, however, identify three core objectives which should guide a player and keep them in arguments for decades. These comprise a) drink as much as possible; b) maintain honour and prestige, and c) cheat and gain advantage over friends through manipulation, hoodwinking and skulduggery.

How to play Passatella, and create arguments for life

Number of players: An even number, four to eight would be ideal.

[xiv] J. Davies, 'Passatella: An Economic Game', p. 199.
[xv] Russell L. Langworthy, 'The Peasant World View', p. 214.

You will need:
- Wine. This is insisted on by players of Passatella in nineteenth-century Rome, but in twentieth-century rural Sicily beer seemed to do just fine, provided you called it *vino*.
- A close-knit, thick-skinned argumentative bunch of friends you know very well and all of whom are prepared for a lifetime of game-layering, debt-building and blush-inducing skulduggery.
- Time, preferably days, weeks, months and years of real-life connection and relationships, so the game can flow with and bend around your very own alliances, arguments, betrayals, debts and forgiving.
- Finally, a pack of cards, a lot of sticks, dice or even rock, paper, scissors to decide who are the *padrones* each round. For best results use a traditional Neapolitan pack of playing cards.

How to play:
1. Each round, play a simple hand of cards (or equivalent) to determine two *padrones*, bosses or masters. Set out fewer glasses than players and fill them with *vino*.
2. The two masters have total control of the *vino* allotted to this match. One of the masters must make a proposal to the other, or debate who starts the proposals, of who of the group should drink.
3. The other master, who should have or quickly create divergent interests and relationships to their fellow master, should reject or deny each of the proposed drinker proposals based on their game friends and the pre-existing (borrowed, or imagined) debts, betrayals, bonds and obligations they have among the players and then make counterproposals of ever-increasing outrageousness on who should drink.

4. Eventually, and after much wild accusation, insult, divulging of rude truths, bargaining, denial and deliberation, some players will finally be without drink while others will be given drink by the masters. It is possible but rare for the masters to drink the allocation entirely themselves as to do so is to make no friends, create no returns nor create new debts among the players and thus will likely limit your access to *vino* in future rounds.
5. The group, which will now be merrily quarrelling, insulting and jibing, often at the players without *vino* (the ulmos), can then quench their thirst. Though at any time the masters can deny a player to drink, to sip or otherwise in that round. Any player too can bargain with another and will gain further credit if they in some way manage to outwit, double-cross or enrage their bargain partner; for they will be *furbo*, skilful and cunning.
6. The play will then begin again, once drinks are finished and egos bruised, with scores, crucially, eternally unsettled – each broken promise, insult and denial, each offer and obligation a layer of complexity to draw on as you forever play Passatella.

Top tip: do not forget, but also do not abuse, the trait of *furbo* (to be cunning) in gameplay. It's a fine balance to feel one's way to where bending and breaking the rules to outfox your friends is in the spirit of the game and celebrated; or where it breaks the form totally and ruins the efforts of you and your peers. You will have to find out for yourself.

Scientific Sipping

*Astronomy, Automata and Alcohol in
Aristocratic Germany, 1400–1750* CE

German beer hall culture is legendary, with Oktoberfest fast becoming an unavoidable commercial event. It has spawned a plethora of invented German traditional-style games to keep revellers entertained. Think hammering nails into logs, Maßkrug glass balancing and brat balancing and other a-historical merriment.

Though Oktoberfest draws on cultural imagery of an old and much romanticised Germany, it is actually a fairly recent tradition, originating from a five-day festival in Munich put on in 1810 by the Bavarian crown prince to celebrate his marriage. Naturally culminating in a horse race, the event proved so popular that the year after saw races put on again, aligned with the local farming show.

Going back further into the German past, when the Renaissance and Reformation shaped a religious and scientific revolution across the German-speaking and wider European world, you find a range of quirky drinking game traditions for Germanic high society at weddings, at princely courts and on hunting getaways. Much to Martin Luther's despair that Germany's 'plague' would forever be a thirst for boozing,[i] these games were usually a form of one-upmanship showing off wealth, prestige and the command of master craftsmen, as nobles collected these unusual drinking games for their *Kunstkammer* (art or curiosity room), usually some kind of boozy automata, highly prized and expensive drinking vessels embedded with clockwork mechanisms to move them in amusing ways on the dinner table.

These rather silly automaton were the marvel of high society across Europe in this period, and rumours abounded of the mechanical wonders the rich were developing in increasingly tall tales. One apocryphal example of an automaton commissioned by the Bishop of Naples suggested that his automaton of a large brass fly was municipally employed, scattering every single fly from the streets and food stalls of Naples for eight years, during which time no food in the city rotted.[ii] Yet it was in the German-speaking world, where many of the artisans producing these machines

---

i Nina Martyris, 'The Other Reformation: How Martin Luther Changed Our Beer, Too', *NPR Illinois*, 31 October 2017.
ii Silvio A. Bedini, 'The Role of Automata in the History of Technology', *Technology and Culture*, vol. 5, no. 1 (Winter, 1964), p. 31.

were based, where automata took on a bizarre and particularly boozy role in courtly drinking games.

A history of Germany and drink without Germany

Germany in the fifteenth and sixteenth centuries didn't exist: when we say Germany what we really mean in this period is a collection of German-speaking kingdoms, principalities and other small states which were independent of one another politically but shared a common Germanic culture and identity while being ruled within the Holy Roman Empire.

German states grew in wealth, status and power as the Renaissance in northern Germany saw the Lutheran Reformation and revolution, where Protestantism broke away from the Catholic Church. Protestantism was liberated in part due to its embrace of a breakthrough invention, the printing press, which enabled Luther and other rebel priests to print religious texts in the vernacular (rather than in Latin), beginning with Gutenberg's Bible. German state rulers were increasingly faced with a choice: to follow the Reformation as it took hold and break away from the Catholic world or to renounce Protestantism and remain in the orbit of Rome. States nearer the epicentre of Luther's religious earthquake, in Wittenberg, Saxony, tended to break away while southern German states followed their population's steadfast loyalty to Catholicism.

The earthquake of the Reformation didn't only shake up the religious order, it also changed the taste of beer for ever. Monasteries, controlled by the Catholic Church, were keepers of the traditional beer-making techniques in much of Germany and they used a mix of exclusive herbs, spices and know-how to flavour their beer and keep their beers superior to those made outside the monastery by lay-folk. The use of this mixture was tightly controlled but ordinary people had experimented with a common German weed, the hop, to flavour their beers. The Catholic Church hated the use of hops, according to a proclamation by the German mystic Hildegard, who said hops were bad for people as 'they make the soul of a man sad and weigh down his inner organs'. As a result, thirsty Protestants used every opportunity to shun the Catholic Church, including through the use of said hops as a beer flavouring, a flavour that increasingly proved better and more popular.[iii]

Luther himself was a fan of the hopped brew. He praised the hoppy beer from Torgau, calling it finer than wine, and even credited it for his sleep, stating, 'I sleep six or seven hours running, and afterwards two or three. I am sure it is owing to the beer.' His wife, Katharina von Bora, brewed beer that became so popular it was a staple in their home. Luther's affection for beer was so well known that when he married Katharina, the town council gifted them a barrel of excellent Einbeck beer. So, thanks to Luther, the Reformation didn't just change theology – it also changed the taste of beer for ever.[iv]

With so many Germanic states and royal courts, skilled artisans had a great number of patrons to sell their wares to, and trends and fads among princes and courtiers were common. Patronage was often religious, particularly as state leaders sought to reflect or repress the changing religious allegiances in

---

iii Nina Martyris, 'The Other Reformation'.
iv Nina Martyris, 'The Other Reformation'.

the aftermath of the Reformation. Yet princes are inevitably lovers of gadgetry and trinkets for themselves too, and none more so than in their fascination with mathematics, astronomy and instruments used to calculate the movements of the stars, a pastime which was hugely popular among German-speaking royals in the second half of the sixteenth century. The French philosopher Petrus Ramus wrote how fortunate Germany was for its mathematically inclined royals, noting 'to what degree the princes of Hesse, Saxony and Austria have become captivated by the study of mathematics'.[v]

Arguably a well-intentioned hobby, this interest led to a proliferation of skilled clock-making artisans developing a range of instruments, clocks and automata across what is now modern-day Germany, with centres of excellence in the states of Nuremberg and Augsburg. The interest in clockwork in this period drove advances in clock-making technology, but it also seems to have driven some of these skilled artisans to distraction, pushed to their limits by mathematically crazed princes. The account by Ambriosio Morales describes one clockmaker, Gianello Torriano, who was tasked by Emperor Charles V (Holy Roman Emperor and Archduke of Austria from 1519 to 1556), to reproduce a clockwork celestial model with over 1,800 individual cogs which took twenty years just to conceptualise. It then took him a further three and a half years to build the machine, during which he was taken so ill with the stress he nearly died.[vi]

---

[v] Bruce T. Moran, 'Princes, Machines and the Valuation of Precision in the 16th Century', *Sudhoffs Archiv*, Bd. 61, H. 3 (1977, 3. QUARTAL), pp. 209–28, p. 209

[vi] Bruce T. Moran, 'Princes, Machines and the Valuation of Precision in the 16th Century', p. 214.

All work and no play makes a prince a dull royal and 'twas ever thus, even in this astronomically interested amalgamation of German-speaking royal courts. When princes were not stargazing, taking sides in religious and political conflict or otherwise extorting and exercising control over their subjects, they liked, as all do, to entertain. A proliferation of clockwork artisans, princes, money and wine came together to create an arms race of alternative automata, not for studying the stars but for dazzling guests at banquet tables, and engaging in one-upmanship with their princely rivals. Increasingly, clockmakers learned the techniques of the jeweller and vice versa, so these bizarre drinking instruments became more ornate, more ostentatious and more outrageous to satisfy the tastes of each court.

Automated alcohol

German drinking culture offered princes a range of intoxicants to draw upon with which to quench their table guests, including beer varieties we might recognise today originating from monastic brewing as early as 1000 CE. Equally, royals and royal guests could sample from a strong tradition of winemaking dating back as far as the Romans, with traditions kept and cultivated again in monasteries throughout the medieval period when German 'noble sweet' wines were prized alongside French claret as the best of the best, both in and outside of the German-speaking world. Men who couldn't hold their drink in society were largely derided, which was a key foundation of the drinking games that emerged, to humiliate the lightweight and reward the heavy drinker.

Combine clockwork wizardry, prized German wine and royal patronage and you get drinking game automata: ornate machines and vessels designed to delight, confound and inebriate guests of high society. A range of these fancy table ornaments survive today in collections across the world and each reveals the secrets of the courtly drinking games they enabled.

One example from the British Museum collection depicts a hunter and dog striding into a forest on a boar hunt. Leaves and newts cover the forest floor in the most delicate of silver work while the moustached hunter carries a pike and is suited and booted in fine brocade and ruff. A fine ornament worthy of any table's centrepiece, and yet beneath its base hides a clockwork mechanism of precise detail. Made in Nuremberg by Wolf Christoff Ritter in around 1617, the ornament hides a hollow interior, indeed capped by the huntsman's noble head; for the ornament is in fact a bottle. When the mechanism was wound, the huntsman would advance along a table, perhaps clattering or gliding, until it came to a stop and where it rested the spear's point would indicate who at the table would drink the entire contents of the hunter. Likely used in uproarious hunting lodge banquets, it would've been incumbent on the guests to hold their drink and make merry at the table of their host – and this unruly drink randomiser would delight and damn those drunken guests.

Another example, now in New York's Metropolitan Museum of Art, was made in Augsburg in 1620. In this clockwork drinking trophy, Diana, goddess of the hunt, rides a huge stag, golden and sporting the antlers that Renaissance deerstalkers could only dream of bagging. Hunting dogs which might mirror those lying beneath the banquet hall's tables stand attentive beneath the stag's hollow body. When filled with wine or spirit (perhaps *Kirschwasser*, a strong cherry brandy) and wound, Diana would again ride forth across the table to one unwitting drinker, who would down the lot or face social ruin at the table.[vii]

> A further and even less understood drinking ornament was also a craze in this period, that of the table fountain. Originating first in Byzantine and Muslim courts, table fountains caught on in this period in Flemish, French and German courts. The few that survive bear little witness to how they were used but it's possible they spouted rosewater, wines or other liquids to delight, cleanse or distract guests at banquet tables. It's clear they too were part and parcel of the complex drinking game paraphernalia of the great European Renaissance feasts.

Automata weren't the only objects keeping the party going in German high society in this period. Even without clockwork mechanisms to confuse guests, the craftiest of novelty drinking vessels designed as table ornaments were being painstakingly made to mock the guests of society by craftsmen in this period. A hollow silver stag, for example, which can only be poured without spilling by holding it

---

vii Joachim Friess, Diana and the Stag, c. 1620, silver, German, Augsburg, The Metropolitan Museum of Art, New York, Accession Number 17.190.746.

upside down might catch out an unwitting diner and embarrass them at table. Vessels shaped as cities, hunting chariots, maidens, dogs, centaurs, chickens, windmills, ships, lanterns, wine carts, fruit, monks, bears, owls, boars, nuns and farmers, unicorns and monks are recorded as having been made for this purpose, some automated, others not, but all designed to titillate and confuse guests, prompting them to spill, spurt or swallow the contents of this bestiary of vessels.

In this period we also find the origin of another traditional, fine-crafted, quirky German drinking vessel still used today: the Maiden's Cup or *Jungfrauenbecher*. Made usually of silver, the cup's form mirrors that of a woman, standing on the table with her dress forming the larger of two goblets, the second of which is a smaller basket held above her head, arms aloft. This second basket pivots and hangs loose so that as the larger cup is turned, it too can turn without spilling its contents. Tradition dictates that at weddings newly-weds take their first married drink from this cup together, with the woman taking the smaller cup. It's said that the first to finish their cup essentially wears the trousers in the marriage. It's also recorded that *Jungfrauenbecher* were used as wager cups more widely in beer halls and taverns, with drinkers challenged to drink from both cups without spilling even a drop.

How to banquet like a clockwork-obsessed Renaissance German prince

Number of players: As many as can fit in your hunting lodge.

You will need:
- A skilled silversmith, jeweller or clockmaker and access to precious metals.
- OR a skilled papier-mâché-smith, plastic bottles, paints and decorating knick-knacks.
- A clockwork or wind-up mechanism (think those wind-up toys you get in crackers).
- *Kirschwasser* (German sour cherry liquor), German wine, beer or other tipples.
- A fine banquet and esteemed guests.

How to play:
1. Having first painstakingly created a range of wind-up, novelty, spill-inducing or otherwise hilarious joke bottles, arrange them, full of liquor, by the side of the banquet.
2. When plied well with food and alcohol and your guests are enjoying a post-dinner belt-loosening, roll out the outrageous, ostentatious and outlandish vessels to the crowd's delight.
3. It will be clear on a point of honour that no guest could refuse your request to pour themselves a drink from the novelty bottle shaped like a Bluetooth speaker, a scented candle or a popular board game (let your imagination run wild with whatever object you might want to make), but guests will laugh with delight as the contents spill and spill as your embarrassed friend mistakes pouring angle after pouring angle before finding that the headphone jack must be the other way up to pour a good measure of its contents without disaster.
4. Turning to your neighbours on the other side of the table you wind up and unleash the disguised clockwork

drinking curiosity, it speeds along the table with aplomb before weakly faltering at a friend's placemat. On their honour they must drink the entire vessel, designed as you see fit, of *Kirschwasser*, fill it and set the penguin on again in its relentless mission to inebriate the table at any cost.

Top tip: the more outlandish the disguise of the confounding drinking vessel the better, but don't skimp on the mechanism which enables the game; go big on the clockwork mechanism.

History Rinsed with Vodka

*(Un)diplomatic Drinking Games in
Russia, 1200 CE–Present Day*

Russian vodka, perhaps the most well-known, notorious spirit in the world, is a drink which has spawned a history to match that reputation. A dance with the devil, Russia's history of alcohol consumption is jarring and sometimes difficult; but vodka is also a source of great national pride, cultural (and literal) strength and the drink of choice for any celebration. From its earliest development in the thirteenth century, to its many nationalisations by different Russian rulers, vodka drinking is entwined in Russian history; from Stalin's sinister, drunken game playing with his cabinet, to the role of vodka as a state money machine and (briefly) an unofficial currency, to the expulsion of vodka distillers in 1917 which led to the West's taste for the tipple. Customs of toasting one's guests (occasionally to excess) have so many rules that one could easily mistake them for a type of game. Yet these welcoming customs help honour both guests and the occasion that brings everyone to the table. While you might imagine neat shots and hard-nosed games, vodka is most commonly consumed when accompanied with delicious food, good company and enthusiasm. There is no one drinking 'game' that defines Russian vodka drinking, so this chapter explores its origins and dark past, vodka's role in game-playing in Russian history and uncovers a few bizarre and apocryphal drinking games that have emerged in Russia.

Russian history distilled

Vodka has played an integral role in the Russian state in one form or another, casting a dark shadow over much of its history; it is also a convivial social lubricant, essential for reunions, guests, celebration and friendship. Though that hasn't stopped some developing some highly unusual drinking games around it; or it being used to play games of another sort entirely, 'great games' of statesmanship, diplomacy and deceit.

Russian drinking is of course synonymous with vodka, a clear high-proof spirit distilled from grains or potatoes. Ranging from 40 to 55 per cent ABV (or stronger still if home-made), vodka has a subtle, sometime almost unnoticed taste profile and is notable for being best enjoyed at below 0 degrees, where it is still liquid.

Russia's relationship with alcohol is difficult too. The state's founding religious myth is that Christianity was chosen in 988 to be the state's creed by Prince Vladimir of Kievan Rus because of Islam's teetotal rules, and even as late as 2013 beer was officially classed as a soft drink. In making that choice in 998, the prince, according to Nestor's chronicle, allegedly exclaimed, 'Drinking ... is the joy of the Russes. We cannot exist without,'[i] a proclamation that would for the centuries ahead at least appear to ring true.

Vodka's origin, whether Polish or Russian, is disputed and mercifully difficult to establish, but we can be certain it developed after distillation techniques, which were first advanced in the Middle East for the distillation of perfumes and oils for Muslim rulers during the Islamic Golden Age as early as the ninth century CE, reached Europe and were quickly put to nefarious use strengthening local tipples.

V. V. Pokhlebkin's history of Vodka gives a definitive start date for 'Russian Vodka' in 1430, though references to 'bread wine', burnt wine and distilled wine suggest it was being made at least a century earlier. By 1545 vodka was evidently so popular and widely drunk that Ivan the Terrible banned the free trade of alcohol entirely and replaced it with a 'nationalised' network of '*kabaks*', franchised vendors who tax-farmed vodka sales, returning profits to the Russian treasury, a system that lasted until 1863.[ii]

---

i Ilkka Henrik Mäkinen and Therese C. Reitan, 'Continuity and Change in Russian Alcohol Consumption from the Tsars to Transition', *Social History*, 31.2 (2006), p. 164.
ii Ilkka Henrik Mäkinen and Therese C. Reitan, 'Continuity and Change in Russian Alcohol Consumption from the Tsars to Transition', p. 164.

Under Tsar Peter the Great (1672–1725) a reliance on vodka was pressured onto the Russian population as a means of control, with rules preventing wives from removing husbands forcibly from *kabaks* and allowing problem drinkers in debtors' prison reprieve through twenty-five years of service in the army. Serfs, too, were cajoled and forced into vodka drinking, with landowners paying wages in vodka – all proceeds to the benefit of the state. One serf, upon his freeing, opened a tiny vodka tavern in Moscow, and Pyotr Smirnov's tavern would later grow into a popular Russian brand which at the turn of the twentieth century was producing a quality vodka.[iii] This practice of state profit on the sale of alcohol grew and grew; by 1859, just before the end of serfdom, vodka accounted for 40 per cent of ordinary revenues of the Russian state, over 120 million roubles.[iv]

Vodka drinking became a remarkable feature of Russian life, most prominently in towns and cities (1858 figures suggest St Petersburg drank a whopping 25 litres per capita) but also in the countryside, where it was a part of the rhythm of rural life.[v] Pressure from the state to indulge wasn't the only driver, however. Russian peasant life was filled with opportunities to delight in Russian traditions, most particularly on religious holidays, secular holidays, family events, when hosting and during business transactions. Orthodox

iii Heidi Brown, 'Drinking Games: Can Russia Admit It Has a Problem?', *World Policy Journal*, 28.2 (2011), p. 116.
iv David Christian, 'Vodka and Corruption in Russia on the Eve of Emancipation', *Slavic Review*, 46.3 (1987), p. 471.
v Ilkka Henrik Mäkinen and Therese C. Reitan, 'Continuity and Change in Russian Alcohol Consumption from the Tsars to Transition', p. 164.

feast days, celebrated with the spirit, amounted to a third of the calendar year and when not religiously engaged, pagan festivals, the annual draft of men to the army, weddings and the end of harvest were equally good reasons to raise a glass, though dry season before harvest was a time of abstinence. Dr Bulovskii's evidence to the 1895 anti-alcohol congress gave more detail on the ubiquity of drunkenness in Russia's rural culture:

> In the villages they drink only after working hours, and at marriages, baptisms, Easter, Christmas and other religious holidays and at fair [. . .] The rest of the time they drink considerably less.[vi]

Cracking down on alcohol

Things got so bad by the start of the twentieth century that the already unpopular Tsar Nicholas II banned alcohol entirely during the First World War (having nationalised vodka in 1904) to reduce violence, poverty and preserve grain and potatoes, and presumably to sober up otherwise drunken workers for the war effort. However, the measure was highly unpopular and according to the *British Medical Journal*'s correspondent in 1915, had little success either:

> There has been a disquieting increase of illicit distillation and resort to the use of methylated spirit as a beverage. Dr Novoselsky has given reasons for thinking that the mortality

---

[vi] Patricia Herlihy, 'Joy of the Rus': Rites and Rituals of Russian Drinking', *The Russian Review*, 50.2 (1991), p. 138.

from drunkenness in Petrograd has developed in inverse proportion to the intensity of prohibitive measures.[vii]

The failure of the measure's success and the contempt it caused among the general population, not to mention the impact on the state's finances, caused severe problems for the tsar's ailing regime, fanning a far wider and deep-rooted discontent which would culminate in the Bolshevik Revolution of 1917. The crackdown of the tsar and then the Bolsheviks, however, did have consequences that are still felt today in the vodka-sphere, as it forced several distillers to flee Russia and establish their vodka businesses in Europe and, later, the United States, including the then popular tipple made by former serf Pyotr Arsenievich Smirnov and his son Vladimir. Despite being a favourite distiller of the Romanovs, the Smirnovs were put out of business by the 1904 nationalisation of vodka and Vladimir fled Russia in 1917, establishing a vodka distillery first in Constantinople, then in modern-day Ukraine and later in Paris in 1925 under the more anglicised name 'Smirnoff'. It was only in 1933, on selling Smirnoff's rights in post-Prohibition America to a Russian distiller in Connecticut, that Vladimir set Smirnoff on course to become the world's most widely drunk and recognisable vodka.[viii]

After the Russian Revolution, the principle of prohibition was one of the few continuations with the Romanov regime, with alcohol distilleries closed after the takeover of the

[vii] 'The Russian Vodka Monopoly', *British Medical Journal*, 2.2855 (18 September 1915), pp. 44–45.
[viii] Heidi Brown, 'Drinking Games: Can Russia Admit It Has a Problem?', p. 116.

revolutionaries. Yet perhaps unsurprisingly, this didn't last and in the battle for Russia which followed in the civil war years it proved not only difficult to enforce the ban (as Russians made their own more dangerous alternatives), but also expensive and unpopular. By 1920 the ban was no longer enforced, with the lucrative vodka receipts flowing substantially into the Kremlin once again. From the ban's dissolving in around 1920 to its collapse in 1991, vodka was a huge financial contributor to the USSR state coffers, with taxes from the spirit representing 13 per cent of the total budget of 1929–30 and still 10 per cent of Soviet revenue in 1989. For comparison, in 2024–2025 alcohol duties in the United Kingdom equated to 1.1 per cent of all state receipts.[ix]

Though the flag had changed, many of the state-induced drinking policies re-emerged or were revived. Stalin in the Second World War mandated the provision of '100 grams of courage'[x] a day to his soldiers, a measure of vodka to keep morale up in the appalling conditions of the Eastern Front and once more embedding a reliance on vodka among many of those soldiers who survived the war. The USSR government also invested in the development of synthetic ethanols to make 'vodka' in the 1950s, in an attempt to preserve limited supplies of potatoes and grain for food; however, this was supposedly stopped in 1963 when it was declared too toxic for human consumption, though rumours of this practice continuing can be found.[xi]

---

ix Office for Budget Responsibility, *Alcohol Duties*, October 2024.
x Heidi Brown, 'Drinking Games: Can Russia Admit It Has a Problem?', p. 117.
xi William Alex Pridemore, 'Heavy Drinking and Suicide in Russia', *Social Forces*, 85.1 (September 2006), p. 493.

Contemporary studies of the 1970s USSR showed the scale of drinking in Russian society, with *Pravda* reporting 'drinking bouts lasting many days and involving large numbers of people and in which an unhealthy competition in plying the guests with liquor has been conducted'.[xii] The authorities tried to reduce consumption in the 1970s, given the social ills the widespread reliance on vodka caused, closing some 18 per cent of alcohol producers for unsanitary conditions, yet reliance prevailed. In the 1980s the practice of 'killing the whole bottle' was encouraged by the fact that state-monopolised alcohol companies marketed vodka with only a plastic or tin cap which was not re-sealable once the bottle had been opened.[xiii] One 1980s Soviet joke makes light of a dark truth about the effects of vodka on the population in remote parts of the union: Brezhnev gets a telegram from Siberia – 'Quick, send two train cars of vodka. The people have sobered up and are asking where the Tsar is.'[xiv]

Efforts to reduce vodka drinking by closing off the supply mostly drove individuals to produce their own home distilled '*samogon*', which was often stronger and also less pure, with some additives like tobacco, gasoline and burnt rubber used to give it that special something.

The 1990s saw a further rise in alcohol use, in part due to the turmoil and exploitation of Russia during the transition from a communist economy: the removal of a state monopoly on alcohol in 1992 meant the state did not collect duties

---

[xii] Walter D. Connor, 'Alcohol and Soviet Society', *Slavic Review*, 30.3 (1971), p. 570.
[xiii] Pridemore, 'Heavy Drinking and Suicide in Russia', p. 491.
[xiv] Heidi Brown, 'Drinking Games: Can Russia Admit it Has a Problem?', p.111.

and, as a result, prices plummeted. At the same time, there was an influx of international companies, which led to increased supply and alternative alcohols from overseas becoming available, with many citing alcohol as a major factor in the decline in life expectancy.[xv]

> *Samogon* literally translates as 'distillate made by oneself'.[xvi]
>
> Today, *samogon* is legal and a popular hobby which many Russians take part in. A still is required and then a mash (a heated mass of squashed ingredients for the alcohol) using sugar (from starchy foods like millet, fruit, potato, wheat, beetroot or even old jam or compote); water and yeast are left to ferment for two weeks and then distilled once the hard 'head and tail' of undrinkable spirit are removed, and its then re-distilled a further time.[xvii]

During this period vodka became more than simply a drink of great importance to Russians, it also became a currency for transactions, particularly for those who used the collapse of the Russian state to take whatever they could to survive. One journalist's travels in Russia noted that

---

xv Jay Bhattacharya, Christina Gathmann and Grant Miller, 'The Gorbachev Anti-Alcohol Campaign and Russia's Mortality Crisis', *American Economic Journal: Applied Economics*, 5.2 (2013), p. 238.

xvi Jay Bhattacharya, Christina Gathmann and Grant Miller, 'The Gorbachev Anti-Alcohol Campaign and Russia's Mortality Crisis', p. 238.

xvii Sorokina, 'Russian Moonshine: What is Samogon?', *Russia Beyond*, 23 October 2019.

villagers purchased vodka over and above their ability to purchase ordinary foods; but far from fulfilling negative stereotypes of drunk Russians it proved in fact that these bottles provided an exchange reserve for future bartering needs in the absence of a stable currency. For example, a woman owning some pigs might pay for their slaughter by a butcher with two bottles of vodka, or someone might purloin a ton of manure from a state farm on her behalf and plough it into her plot for a further two bottles. In one case at a state carrot farm, lorry drivers transporting the produce were known to swap bags of carrots in exchange for vodka between leaving the field and reaching the farm's bean counters.[xviii]

Today, increased regulation is bringing the rate of problem alcoholism down in Russia, and while the reputation for heavy drinking still exists it's a difficult stereotype for many Russians. For most, vodka remains a social celebrant enjoyed traditionally and moderately with Russian food, pastimes and good company.

Playing games with drinkers

We've already seen the cruel gaming of state financing through the sale of alcohol throughout Russian history, but Russian rulers also liked to play the 'great game' of diplomacy with something strong to help it go down. Stalin played drinking games with allies, colleagues and enemies alike; Milovan Djilas, a Yugoslavian politician, wrote of a

---

[xviii] Myriam Hivon, 'Vodka: The "Spirit" of Exchange', *The Cambridge Journal of Anthropology*, 17.3 (1994), pp. 1–18.

game held in Stalin's dacha in 1948 where each attendee had to guess the degrees below zero it was outside and had to down a shot for each degree off they were from the actual temperature. Beria reportedly missed by three degrees.[xix]

Stalin's cabinet, the Politburo, was also victim to his drinking games as he would ply them with alcohol and play them off against one another, securing his position and unsettling theirs as they bent to his demands that they drink more and then squirmed as he challenged and scrutinised them and encouraged them to fight among themselves. Khrushchev, who would eventually succeed Stalin in the battle for power after his death, aptly remarked that only Stalin ever had fun at these 'parties'.

Stalin was an entertainer of diplomats of all stripes, lavishing visiting dignitaries with banquets and also weakening them with games of drinking endurance. Welcoming the Nazi delegation in 1939 to sign an infamous non-aggression pact, the Soviet foreign minister proposed a toast to each of the twenty-two delegates in attendance before a celebratory dinner, and then afterwards proposed to drink to each of the delegation members who were not in attendance too. Stalin later confided to the sozzled Germans that his glass for each of the toasts had contained a delightfully light Crimean wine rather than neat vodka.[xx]

Churchill was treated to the same raucous hospitality, which it's reported he proved a good match to. Foreign

[xix] Chris Hall, 'Getting Pickled with Joseph Stalin', *JSTOR Daily*, 10 January 2024.
[xx] Mark Lawrence Schrad, 'The Vodka Effect: Happy New Year – A Short History of Booze Diplomacy', *Politico Magazine*, 30 December 2013.

Office papers record a visit to the Kremlin in 1942 which led to a night of strong drinking between him and the Georgian dictator during a dinner (and drinks) meeting lasting from 7 p.m. until 3 a.m. After consuming 'innumerable bottles', Churchill was complaining only of a 'slight headache' by 1 a.m., when no doubt panicking officials came to rescue him, but he was wisely at that point sipping an 'innocuous' Caucasian red wine.[xxi] It was reported in dispatches that this placed the British leader on a good footing with the Georgian, who had a preference to negotiate with strong drinkers.

Charles de Gaulle, on the other hand, got a series of thirty toasts on his visit towards the end of the Second World War, with each one increasingly alarming in its sentiment, such as 'To Air Force Commander Aleksander Novikov: a good Marshal, let's drink to him. And if he doesn't do his job properly, we'll hang him!' Novikov was sent to the gulag just two years after the toast. Stalin later assured the French president-in-exile that though called a monster, he liked to make a joke of it.[xxii] De Gaulle still may have got off lightly, however: US envoy Wendell Willkie's wartime visit to Moscow reportedly involved fifty-three vodka toasts at the state dinner put on in his honour.[xxiii]

This state-sponsored game of over-toasting dignitaries (often to gain tactical advantage) hasn't gone away since the

---

xxi 'Churchill and Stalin Made "Merry" Until Early Hours', *BBC News*, 23 May 2013.
xxii Mark Lawrence Schrad, '*The Vodka Effect*'
xxiii John M. Jordan, 'A Small World of Little Americans: The $1 Diplomacy of Wendell Willkie's One World', *Indiana Magazine of History*, 88.3 (September 1992), p. 184.

fall of the USSR. In 2013 the US political magazine *Politico* recounted the case of a US General on a working group mission to Moscow who received undue attention due to his rather extreme reaction to Russia's famous hospitality. During the course of an initial banquet, US delegates were reportedly treated to nine rounds of vodka toasts; at a more lavish banquet the following day this grew to twenty-five rounds of toasts, including some rather ill-considered toasts added by the US general, such as one related to Syria's conflict and another to Edward Snowden. The general was 'found' the following morning after an evidently lengthy night of cultural exchange in Moscow's bars and was later dismissed from service. The head of the Russian delegation was reputed to be toasting with water.[xxiv]

Drink like an ordinary Russian instead

However, as infamous as these examples are, they shouldn't cast a shadow over the traditional yet unbeautiful ritual of the Russian toast. Vodka, brought out to celebrate, welcome, commiserate or mark an occasion, should never be drunk alone and should be accompanied with *zakuski* – cold snacks, such as salty fish, or salad bites. After each glass is downed (always in one) it is traditional to sniff or eat a piece of salted bread – the sniffing originated when there was not enough bread to go around. If one has no bread at all, it remains a custom to sniff one's sleeve.

Several other traditions come with the gregarious custom of Russian toasting: that alcohol is poured to all

---

[xxiv] Mark Lawrence Schrad, *'The Vodka Effect'*

those present, that one can never toast with an empty glass, nor should an empty bottle be placed on the table. Glasses should be filled only on a surface and pouring should be transparent with one hand on the side of the bottle to allow those present to ensure only vodka enters the glass. Revellers should touch glasses as every toast is drunk in all cases bar funerals and commemorations, which are more solemn affairs. There should be no long gap between the first and second toasts, nor should a late-coming guest avoid the earlier drinks poured by the host – they would be given to them in addition to their welcome glass upon their arrival. Upon leaving, guests are invited to take a *na pososhok*, literally a walking stick 'for the road'. A common toast, among many, remains the immortal words of cosmonaut and first human in space Yuri Gagarin – '*Poyekhali!*' ('Let's go!') – which he uttered as he was launched into orbit.

Largely inadvisable historical Russian drinking games

While toasting, either as a tussle of the highest diplomatic stakes or simply in accordance with its many rules, might seem game enough in Russian history, a host of other drinking games have developed too. Many of them are apocryphal, with little written record of their precise origins or rules, but some accounts survive, including:

Trains and Bridges In 1909 an account from a professor complained how a new custom of drinking on trains had developed in a game form where drinks must be taken at every bridge and each crossing. Wryly, he observed that drinkers would, on occasions where a significant interval between crossings occurred, observe that bridges had not yet been built at this point but they should drink anyway.[xxv]

Durak, literally meaning fool, perhaps Russia's most popular card game, is played as a drinking game with the loser (the *durak*) having to drink a glass of vodka for their troubles.

Stairs is not a drinking game well evidenced in record but is said to have been played by Russian teenagers in the 1980s and 1990s and is based on Soviet panel apartment blocks which are in part characterised by having nine-step stairways between each storey. A player ascends the staircase and on each step drinks a cap of vodka, and then repeats with the last still climbing declared the winner.

Bear Paw. In this absurd game, which is reportedly Russian though sources are patchy, a glass of beer is shared by a group who each sip from the glass in turn. After each sip of beer is drunk, a shot of vodka is returned to the glass, and in the following pass round the group the liquid drunk is replaced with beer, and the next round vodka and so on. This seems so far removed from pleasure, skill or fun that one cannot call it a game at all.

How to game drinking, Russian style

Number of players: A crowd enough for a good time.

How to play: Don't. Just don't replicate any of this, especially fifty-three vodka toasts or mean-spirited spirit pushing.

---

xxv Patricia Herlihy, 'Joy of the Rus', p. 143.

How to play (an alternative): Instead, take on the traditional Russian toast with its many rules and gregarious hospitality as a game in and of itself, making toasts of celebration and thankfulness to be enjoyed with friends, families and a spread of delightful Russian foods to ease the burn of good-quality vodka.

You may need:
- Smoked mackerel, salmon or pickled herring.
- Traditional black bread or boiled potatoes with dill.
- Russian cheeses, radishes and capers.
- Blinis, Russian salad and game meats.
- Good-quality Russian vodka.

> **Top tip:** wherever you toast with vodka, sniff your sleeve if there is no food and pick up bonus points, though better still bring the 'bread' to share with your fellow toasters. If you have to make many toasts, don't forget the sneaky craft of the Russian delegation chair in the 1990s; vodka, after all, is visually indistinguishable from water.

Bragging a Horn-full

*Drinking Games and Viking-ing in
Medieval Scandinavia, 750–1200 CE*

Viking isn't the most accurate term for the innovative, seafaring and complex Scandinavian civilisation of warbands and chieftains who built a shared medieval culture that is now legendary, but it is certainly the most well-known term. The act of Viking (in a literal sense) means to undertake a seafaring, warring raid of piracy; it does not refer to a whole group of peoples. Today historians have settled on Norse, Northmen or medieval Scandinavians.

Nonetheless, the medieval communities of Scandinavia (spanning roughly 750–1200 CE) and their extraordinary achievements, crossing the North Atlantic to settle the

Faroe Islands, Iceland, Greenland and Newfoundland (arriving in North America some 400 years before the next European visitor), will likely remain best known by a popular (and false) imagining of bearded, ocean-going bandits in (unreal) horned helmets, rather than the intricate societies they founded or the material and literary legacies they left behind.

Sending shivers down the spines of coastal medieval communities across Europe, there is a case that there is no smoke without fire (including fire from razed and brutalised coastal monasteries), but the historical legacy of the Norse holds much more than it is often credited for (usually just pillaging). The Norse were a complex and gregarious society, capable of advanced technological prowess and strategic vision to settle the icy islands of the North Atlantic; they were efficient and tactical warriors as well as poets, and they were drinkers too.

In the sagas (Norse epic literature), myths and legends of the frozen north we see glimpses of uproarious feasting, great heroes challenging one another and dynasties passing traditions on from one generation to the next through, you guessed it, drinking games. From poetic insult battles to bone throwing, swimming and drowning contests and competitive crowd-rousing, there is ample evidence that the Norse/Vikings had more than enough time for a good time while also terrorising the coasts of Northern Europe and exploring the edges of the known world.

To do a Viking

The groups collectively seen as Norsemen were initially spread across modern-day Denmark, Sweden and Norway. There was no single 'Viking society', as is popularly imagined, but rather a patchwork of clans of tough farming communities able to organise themselves into hard-nosed and fearsome warriors in defence of their own. The societies of the Northmen were varied, shaped by geographical realities and their relations with their neighbouring warbands, but broadly society could be split into three classes: the aristocratic Jarls; the Karls, who were ordinary working folk; and the Thralls, who were people captured and put to work, often forcibly, in the service of the aristocracy.

Like many societies, the Northmen had a range of tipples to suit the most extravagant to the most modest of pockets. Alcohol production, though, was complicated by the limited sources of glucose (and sun) available in the far north, with grain (usually barley) grown only in the south of Scandinavia and distillation techniques not yet having reached the north of Europe.

Ever more innovative, the Northmen used what they had to produce mead (fermented honey wine), beer from barley where it grew and Skyr, if you were unlucky enough to live where bees and barley did not (like Iceland and Greenland), an alcoholic drink from fermented milk that was left for two years. Those who lived where fruits grew also made fruit wines, and the most prized of all drinks were imported wines. Odin, king of the Norse gods, drank only wine, for example, and in fact the eye-watering cost of wine in Scandinavia has changed little to this day.

From each region, Norsemen increasingly took to the sea to seek riches, new lands and territories. Bands from modern-day Sweden sought riches in raiding and settling the Baltic; the groups from modern-day Norway headed to the Scottish Isles, the Faroes, Iceland, Greenland and even Newfoundland, and later the Danes crossed the North Sea to England. Other bands headed further east still, up the Volga River and across the Russian steppe; one group crossed the Caspian Sea to visit Baghdad in around 1000 CE. Raiding bands would set out on years-long voyages, often occupying islands offshore as far away as Spain and France, to conduct a series of raids and conquests before returning north. Norsemen rowed up the Seine in 845 to attack Paris and would return again and again to lay siege to the city, occupying the island of Jenfosse in the river in 853 and 856 so as to launch regular raids and provide a home. These island colonies and commercial coastal holdings (such as in Ireland) gave way to a much larger settlement in 865 when the Great Army landed in eastern England and took a huge swathe of territory,[i] establishing the Danelaw, a state on English soil across the north and east in one form or another until 1066.

As occupiers and traders, the Northmen built relatively modest wooden dwellings and traded and cooperated with locals in their domains of control, such as the Danelaw. In mainland Britain, few Viking buildings remain intact. Yet Norse burials, standing stones and grave goods scatter England and Scotland's landscape, and in the Northern Isles and the Isle of Man, where they never truly left, Viking longhouses, carved rune stones and settlements remain

---

i Barry Cunliffe, *Facing the Ocean: The Atlantic and Its Peoples, 8000 BC–AD 1500* (Oxford, 2001) p. 494.

standing. The long shadow of their influence can be seen in the use of Norse language (Norn) in Orkney and Shetland as late as the eighteenth century.[ii]

In northern England one can still see hogback tombs standing alone in ancient graveyards and inside those churches discover eerie Norse rune-carved arches of granite, alien to the graves around them and bookended by stone-carved animals gripping to their ends. In Scandinavia, one can find many more remains of the Northmen's structures, with ship burials, great carved runestones and stone long-houses, as well as quite extraordinary artefacts of swords, helmets, glassware, chess sets and tools showing the range and skill of their civilisation. Skills they also turned to brewing alcohol, even where no grain dared to grow.

Beyond the material (and liquid) remains of the Norsemen, however, lies a literary heritage, beginning with a donation of some 700 Norse-derived words to common English as well as a wealth of myth and legend to interpret in the sagas of the north. The main understanding we have of Norse customs and culture comes from their poetry and mythology: from extraordinary accounts of real voyages of discovery by Norse explorers to accounts of battles and winters survived in frozen lands to the wild and wonderful mythologies of the Norse gods. In these books too we find a pattern of uproarious feasting, game-playing and celebratory drinking in the great halls of the north, drinking brags and bouts both real and divine.

---

ii Barry Cunliffe, *Facing the Ocean*.

The birth of the poets, through mead

It's clear from mythology that alcohol was ritually significant in Norse culture, and none more so than mead, which was considered a godly drink and one that imbued the drinker with poetic skill.

In the ancient sagas the origin story of mead comes from a daring series of thefts, with the drink first created through the spit-based peace negotiations of two warring god-families. Their congealing spit, naturally, birthed a mystic with the highest intelligence called Kvasir whose blood was in fact all mead, and through this blood flowed poetry itself.

Unfortunately, Kvasir was not intelligent enough to avoid murder by dwarves for his blood-mead, and then this precious liquid was stolen again by a giant. Odin, king of the gods, wanted his own share of this bloody-mega-mead and so disguised himself as an eagle and stole the mead from the giant, allegedly seducing the giant's daughter in the process. As Odin escaped from the giant's lair, some of the mead was spilled from his eagle's beak and fell to earth. It was said that the great Norse saga poets were those folk who by luck were struck by drops of falling mead from Odin's beak.

Norse drinking customs

Beyond the wild and winding escapades of the gods in pursuit of blood-mead, we know a lot of drinking also happened in the mortal Norse realms. Booze was a bind which helped keep Norse society together, with shared drinking a way of professing loyalty and signing contracts, from marriage to inheritance. This drinking, along with most other gatherings (and anything else, for that matter), would take place in the hall, the only place to be in Norse society, what with the winter weather and limited fuel for fires. It was in these halls that the very important business of feast-throwing and drinking in honour of a lord or warrior would take place.

The feast, a sometimes days- or weeks-long exhibition of power and hospitality by the host, was a common (if extraordinarily expensive) way of gift-giving and demonstrating respect among the elites of Norse society. A big bouquet for your sister's birthday or a nice dessert to take to your aunt's weekend lunch seems more reasonable now. Great halls designed for this purpose would ring with music, played on bone flutes, bells, stringed instruments and rattles, as well as shields, which were beaten as drums. Such music would be accompanied by other entertainment, including dramatic performances of the old sagas. Drinking was such an integral part of these feasting celebrations that some later sagas show those who did not drink being ostracised from the retinue of their host with some hostility, their lack of involvement seen as an affront.

This binding together of drinkers was done through a (perhaps unhygienic) custom of *sumbl*, a ritual ceremony also known as 'oath cup', where a woman, often related to the host, would share out a ritual drink among the gathering, one sip at a time and from the same glass. It's possible women undertook this as a nod to their perceived magical power, and their role as brewers too. The order of those served would help establish the hierarchy of the gathering, a diplomatic tightrope no doubt decided carefully by the hosting household. In the sagas, this drinking ritual was often accompanied by an oath or vow.

In *Beowulf*, an Anglo-Saxon poem recounting a saga, Queen Wealhtheow is the cupbearer at a *sumbl*, greeting her husband and king, Horthgar, with drink first before serving others in turn. Beowulf the warrior takes an oath through this ceremony of the *bragafull* after being challenged by the Queen to rid her hall, the hall of Heorot, of the evil beast that stalks it.[iii] Oath-making and -keeping, though, could be lower stakes than defending a hall from its dragon enemies; marriages, alliances and other agreements were kept as oaths, and bound often with communal drinking as a shared witness.

For those not rich, battle-famous or influential enough to be invited to the great feasts in the chieftain's hall, they too found a way to enjoy a glass or two after a tough day on the fjords. This took place in the *Skytningar*, a more informal refectory, essentially a pub, where individuals paid their own dues, rather than the quite expensive business of throwing a feast and footing the bill for everyone. As a result, these drinking places attracted the less wealthy looking for a fix, like farmers, merchants and townsfolk. These everyday dives tended to have a pretty bad reputation, the mark of a good time no doubt.

Foreign merchants were often blamed for the noisy impact of these drinking houses on their surroundings, with Snorri's *Olaf's saga* recording how between 1067 and 1093 King Óláfr Haraldsson Kyrri was displeased with the 'drinking bouts in marketplaces about the land as a consequence of the large number of merchants'. Later Norwegian kings also continued to rail against the drunkenness of the

---

iii Joshua Rood, *Drinking With Óðinn: Alcohol and Religion in Heathen Scandinavia* (Reykjavík: 2014), p. 7.

common man, with King Sverrir in 1300 making a speech against the drunkenness of both his people and the troublesome Germans, who had proved such effective merchants that the stronger wine they traded could now be bought at a price equivalent to local ales, causing outrageous drunkenness among townsfolk.[iv]

Drinking games among the Norse

From gods stealing blood-mead from their giant enemies, to warrior chieftains feasting, toasting and oath making in their great halls, Norse society was intertwined with alcohol, often with a rich societal meaning. Yet this seriousness wasn't the only way drinking was done; in fact, a range of less formal and honourable drinking methods exist in the form of Norse drinking games.

Many sagas tell of drinking competitions, including those taking place between guests at feasts in the game of *mannjafnaor*. The game was essentially a bragging match in which men and sometimes women pitted their wits against each other to rank themselves against the rest. Often tasked with debating who was the greater warrior, based on their athleticism or attractiveness or their pre-eminence in a given district or hall, debates were quarrelsome and raucous.

Such preening could quickly turn sour and descend into another drinking game called *senna,* a form of one-on-one competitive insulting before a crowd, often done in exaggerated poetic verse, with horns of ale drunk between verses

---

iv Guerrero Rodriguez, J. F., *Old Norse Drinking Culture* (PhD thesis, University of Leeds, 2015) p. 181.

which turned this rap battle into a drinking match, as the wit of insult and the strength of stomach were tested before the halls. In one example from a saga, three men exchange round after round of *senna*, drinking horns of ale between each battle:

> The king's men listen to the entertainment. And they took Oddr the horns and he quaffed them both. After that Oddr rises up and goes towards them and he realises that they are conquered by the drink and at the same time that they were beyond composing poetry.[v]

Hnùtukast was another drinking game and one probably left to the very end of the evening as it required none of the brazen boasting or eye-watering insults of Mannjafnaor or Senna. In this simple game, guests would take the bones left over from the meal and, agreeing a series of targets that didn't necessarily exclude living ones, take it in turns to launch them, with the least successful no doubt receiving a forfeit, perhaps of drinking yet more again.

Other silly feast- (and we can therefore read drink-) related games litter the sagas left to us by the Norse Skald poets, from swimming competitions and testing duels to competitions where challengers would see who could hold their head longest under water in a barrel. Evidently almost anything in a hall full of ale-addled men could become a drinking game.

---

[v] *Orvar-Odd saga - XXVII*, quoted by Rodriguez in *Old Norse Drinking Culture*, p. 311.

Are we fair to the Norse and their drinking habits?

No doubt the Northmen deserve far greater recognition for their achievements and societal accomplishments than popular history has awarded them. Regarded unhelpfully as a savage band of bearded raiders, we ignore the complexities of their technologies, the grit of their settlement of the frozen islands of the North Atlantic centuries before other European peoples, and we obscure their innovative trading settlements and conquered outposts which changed the face of Europe for ever with the grisly tales of their bloody raids.

In drinking games, however, we perhaps see a flavour of that unfortunate reputation hold true. The bragging and insult-hurling, the bone-throwing and competition remind us of the warrior elements of their society, as would watching a raucous sports team in a pub fill us perhaps with some dismay. Yet the poetic and literary side of these Norse drinking games, if anything like the telling of the sagas which exist today, show another story. These games would let flow an ancient and fearsomely proud literary tradition of achingly beautiful metaphor, stirring oratory and tub-thumping verse, recalling the exploits of Norse heroes, the sights and sounds of lands flung between Newfoundland and Baghdad and the heady calls to the gods of Asgard and the dark giants and other beasts still wandering the frozen north. Whether pillagers or poets, writers or raiders, warriors or myth-weavers, swordsmen or stand-ups, the Norse sagas of old clearly show that the Norsemen knew how to compete when drinking.

How to drink-game as the Norsemen did

Number of players: A great hall-full.

You will need:
- A great hall. A parish hall will do, if pushed, but check the rules on Viking feasts.
- An assembly of tough, big-eating, hard-drinking companions and your retinue.
- Deep pockets, as you, the host, pay for the great feast laid on in a guest's honour:
  o A great hog roast, breads and cheeses
  o Ales, meads and wines and fermented milk drinks
  o A roaring fire (where capacity and fire safety rules allow)
- Bragafull equipment or an oath cup, such as an ornate goblet or carved horn.
- A long winter's evening, to let the games flow merrily, in unruly fashion.

How to play *mannjafnaor*:
1. When your guests are fit and raring from the fine ales and mead you have put on, bring them close to the hearth and invite them to take part in *mannjafnaor*.
2. Guests will source a yardstick, against which would-be champions will measured: perhaps wit, perhaps brawn, perhaps looks or skills, it's up to you.
3. When the measuring quality is agreed, individuals may stand and, poetically, brag as to why they possess, among those present, the greatest manifestation of that particular attribute. It is essential that before each speech is launched the speaker takes comfort from a great horn of

ale or mead and that they must already be quite far gone in that department to ensure a rather boozy quality to the competition.
4. Guests watching will assess the quality of the brag, both in its veracity and in the quality of its making – to what extent it uses great poetic flow or humour or indeed stirs those present with its recounting of tales and exploits to back the claim.
5. As speakers each take their turn, clear performers will emerge while others will be discounted from the running until only a few remain. They may take a further speech to convince the audience of their rightful claim before a decision is made.
6. The winner takes a stand and, of course, a drink, and the game may begin again.

How to play *senna*:
1. Once the fun of *mannjafnaor* is over, the *senna* may begin. In this game, pairs are identified, perhaps those with an existing connection, relationship or rivalry.
2. The pairs take it in turns to poetically and lyrically hurl abuse at each other in a humorous fashion. [Note the need for good, thick-skinned friends at your feast.] The audience must watch on, perhaps engaging, egging on or goading the speaker.
3. Between speeches, speakers may rest and take a draught of strong ale or mead.
4. Play continues until the speakers no longer make sense, lose the audience or descend into such acrimonious confrontation that poetry is totally abandoned.

How to play Hnùtukast:

1. Agree a target, animate or inanimate, among your now quite incoherent guests.
2. Not *that* object. Be considerate.
3. Pick the discarded feast bones from the tables, floor and walls of the hall.
4. In turn throw the bones at the target, rewarding the successful and punishing those off target quite equally, with a drink.

> **Top tip:** don't attempt the underwater barrel breath-holding game in any circumstances and only hit the mead towards the end of the week-long feast.

Something to Wash Down the Pearl?

Drinking like an (Ancient) Egyptian, 3000 BCE –50 CE

Cradled in the verdant strip of green that the River Nile carves through North-East Africa's arid landscapes, the remnants of one of Africa's many great civilisations are today visited by millions from around the world. The astonishing amount of material evidence of Egyptian civilisation, both in Egypt and spread among thousands of museums elsewhere by zealous 'collectors' (or looters), means many people are familiar with some of the basics of Egyptology. Most schoolchildren could explain the process of mummification, like the gruesome detail that the brain was pulled out through the nostrils and placed in a jar with the head of a jackal on it, or that the pyramids were built in great sandstone blocks and smoothed with marble then capped with gold. The more astute might tell you that the Nile flooded each year, re-fertilising the fields and river pastures which gave life to Egypt, and they might also know the tragic story of Cleopatra or the words of Howard Carter finding 'wonderful things' in the tomb of Tutankhamun. Yet much about the life of ordinary Ancient Egyptians remains the preserve of experts; how these people lived, and drank, is as alien to most now as hard labour was to the pharaohs.

Today Egypt is a Muslim majority country, though it has ancient Christian communities, and alcohol is closely licensed and controlled. Egyptian history, however, has its fair share of boozy and bizarre drinking traditions, games and stories – in fact, in ancient times it was considered that drinking alcohol brought you face to face with the gods. God-like animals were given wine, the dead drank with the living and alcohol was mixed in bizarre ritual cocktails for the likely purpose of accessing another realm. Perhaps most incredible was the drinking game festival of 'Tekh' (the annual festival of drunkenness), where Egyptians inebriated themselves in order to dance with and be in the presence of the goddess of fertility and love, Hathor, transgressing societal rules in a mash-up of the holy and the debauched. Professor Joann Fletcher, the celebrated Egyptologist, has, among many subjects, written on Egypt's fascination with alcohol and this chapter draws on her research.

Extremely Ancient Egypt and its drinks

One of the most astonishing things about Ancient Egyptian culture is the great span of time it covered. It was so vast that the builders of the pyramids at Giza lived at a greater distance in time from the last Egyptians than we today live from the end of Ancient Egyptian civilisation. It is simply too lengthy to summarise as many as 300 pharaohs across thirty-one dynasties, in three historic periods between 3100 and 332 BCE. As a result, the end of the Egyptian civilisation, its takeover and interrelation with first Greek and later Roman culture, was totally different from its early origins, though a certain boozy theme of continuity, among others, can be traced between them.

Ancient Egypt's early influences and technologies came from south-western Asia, from the earliest great human civilisations of Babylon and Mesopotamia which had developed the first systems of large-scale farming and construction technologies as well as systems of taxation. In the narrow fertile belt of the Nile Valley, Ancient Egypt developed and advanced these technologies, irrigating the surrounding land and expanding agriculture beyond simple subsistence farming and developing a centralised and organised state. This large-scale agriculture also produced surplus grain, enabling brewing.

After just a few thousand years or so, Egypt was expanding into and controlling land to its south, known as Nubia, and an ever-increasing class of officials were tasked with the administration of a state which was mostly concerned with waging war and building enormous tombs for its rulers and huge temple complexes to worship (and drink) in. Luckily, these officials demonstrated a panache for record-keeping and revenue-raising which provides much of our evidence beyond the stone structures and tombs still standing.

For ordinary Egyptians the Nile was everything: a method of transport, of field fertiliser, a builders' merchants for the mud which made the bricks of their homes. Most lived as farmers, but as society developed increasing numbers of craftspeople were needed, from stonemasons to painters and metalworkers, papyrus makers to mummification experts, as well as brewers and vintners to serve the increasing tastes and trends of the elite.

Alcohol was a daily reality and religious exercise in Ancient Egypt. Beer, or *enket,* as it was known, was an everyday staple, though it would have tasted different to modern beer, with spices and fruits added to create flavour. The labourers working on the Giza pyramids were given a daily ration of ten pints of the stuff to help them through the day. It was brewed into a range of colours, which also denoted the alcohol content of the tipple: red beer was generally of a lower alcoholic content while black or dark beers were often stronger.

The basic ingredient for Ancient Egyptian beer was a form of barley from which they drew sugars essential for brewing (modern beer would use malt extract) through baking the barley into unleavened bread. These bread loaves made of a coarse flour were often damp and known as *cyllestis.* The baking of bread essentially malted the barley into sugars. These loaves once cooked would be added to a pot to brew and then ferment. Sometimes beers were strengthened with dates and honey. The mash was then stomped on in vats to break down its thick contents and strained before being collected and left to rest, allowing sediments to filter down before the final stage.[i]

Once ready, beer jars were capped with clay and then plaster, but this would only keep beer for a short period, perhaps a few days to a week. Beer was a fresh product and hard to transport or keep from spoiling; in surviving texts on funeral arrangements and the afterlife, there is concern about the spoiling of beer.[ii] As a result of the beer's short shelf life, Ancient Egypt built large-scale, almost industrial-style breweries, usually organised alongside sites such as palaces or temples where, as we will see, vast quantities of fresh beer were often needed.[iii]

The unbroken chain of Egyptian rule from c. 3000 BCE was broken in 525 BCE by an invading Persian army which captured Egypt and placed it under Persian rule, though much of its cultural and religious practices were unchanged. The invasion of the Greeks and Macedonians in 323 BCE under Alexander the Great 'liberated' Egypt from this Persian takeover and established a hybrid Greco-Egyptian royal lineage, mixing Egyptian culture with Greek. The Greeks brought wine and other cultural influences but also adopted Egyptian ways. These harmonious (and merry) Greco-Egyptians also merged their drinking styles and gods and held a great parade in honour of both Osiris and Dionysus, the respective Egyptian and

---

i Homebrewers Association, 'Pharaoh Ale: Brewing a Replica of an Ancient Egyptian Beer.'
ii Justin Jennings et al., 'Drinking Beer in a Blissful Mood: Alcohol Production, Operational Chains, and Feasting in the Ancient World', *Current Anthropology*, vol. 46, no. 2 (April 2005), p. 281.
iii Justin Jennings et al., 'Drinking Beer in a Blissful Mood', p. 281.

Greek gods of wine. The first Grecian female pharaoh, Arsinoe, had a hydraulic automaton wine pourer employed in her temple, with vessels inscribed with images of Hathor and Dionysus.

The Egyptian name for wine, '*irep*', was apparently a pun on the sound of overindulgence (a belch).[iv] Sadly, unlike the northern and eastern Mediterranean, Egypt's climate was less suitable for growing grapes and what grape wine was produced was limited to the most wealthy and celebrated. To get hold of their tipple of choice, especially in the royal capital of Memphis, vintners from Lebanon and Syria were brought in to cultivate a wine-growing tradition as early as 3000 BCE. Subsequent rulers, especially the Greek pharaohs no doubt looking for home comforts, went as far as to retrain veteran soldiers to grow wine and created new towns around water sources for the express purpose of winemaking, while a huge amount of wine was imported from Greece and the Levant to meet demand.[v]

Even in the afterlife, significant efforts were made to supply elites with this most precious of liquids. Winemaking scenes were commonly painted on tomb walls in an attempt to guarantee an after-lifetime supply for the occupant. The most wealthy were buried with wine, both grown in Egypt and imported, with some wine jars existing today with wine still inside.[vi]

As grapes were hard to grow, other fruit wines were made using dates, the sap of palms figs or pomegranates, as well as a reddish strengthened wine, *shedeh*. Depending on the

---

iv Joann Fletcher, 'Wine in Ancient Egypt I', *Immortal Egypt* blog.
v Joann Fletcher, 'Wine in Ancient Egypt I'.
vi Joann Fletcher, 'Wine in Ancient Egypt I'.

status of the revellers, it's possible these wines were used for certain drinking games and rituals among Egyptian elites. To assist the ancient consumer with selecting from this (limited) variety, wine labels were simpler to interpret (and better?) than in contemporary life, with surviving labels denoting 'good quality wine', 'very good quality wine', 'sweet' and even 'wine for merry making'.[vii]

Inebriated livers/lovers

The tale of Cleopatra is a tragic and enduring love story and a legend with a certain boozy flavour as a result of the expensive tastes of star-crossed lovers Cleopatra and Mark Antony. Cleopatra was a great strategist, and her involvement with both Mark Antony and his rival Julius Caesar was also an exercise in statecraft, protecting her rule and lineage as best she could against Roman incursion. In their dramatic and legendary dalliance, Cleo and Mark formed their own drinking society, known as the Inimitable Livers ('livers' of life rather than of flesh, one assumes), and the society (which was mostly just the two of them) enjoyed wandering round Alexandria in secret, dressed like ordinary people and engaging the local population in their own private jokes as well as putting on lavish dinners and drinking nights as ostentatious displays of wealth and power. The society has been viewed by some as a debauched sect, but it is likely to have been a cult devoted to the Grecian god of wine, Dionysus. Plutarch writes of it: 'For they had an association called The Inimitable

---

vii Justin Jennings et al., 'Drinking Beer in a Blissful Mood', p. 292.

Livers, and every day they feasted one another, making their expenditures of incredible profusion.'[viii]

In one jape, a bet was laid between the two lovers and rivals in which Cleopatra created the most expensive cocktail in history. Pliny the Elder wrote how Cleopatra liked to mock Antony's gluttonous drinking and eating at these most sumptuous feasts laid on as part of their most exclusive drinking club. She boasted she could spend ten million sesterces (a vast sum) on a dinner and bet that that she would consume it all herself. Antony disagreed that such a thing was possible and accepted the wager.

At the dinner, Cleopatra waited to be brought a bowl of light vinegar (or wine depending on the source), then took a large pearl earring from her lobe (worth ten million sesterces), crushed it and dropped the broken pearl into a cup of the vinegar before drinking it in one and so creating the world's most expensive cocktail and winning the bet.[ix] An earnest procession of classically interested chemists have spent years experimenting to conclude that no vinegar made at that time could in fact dissolve a pearl, and some have suggested the wily Cleopatra might instead have swallowed the pearl in a glass of wine and 'recovered it later' – not quite the renaissance image of Cleopatra we have today.[x]

At the news of Cleopatra's death on 12 August 30 CE, the Roman poet Horace's ode to her death called for a drinking spree in celebration of the passing of the last of the Egyptian rulers and the state of Egypt coming under full control of the

---

viii Plutarch, 'Inimitable Livers', in Perseus Digital Library.
ix Berthold Louis Ullman, 'Cleopatra's Pearls', *The Classical Journal*, vol. 52, no. 5 (2025).
x Berthold Louis Ullman, 'Cleopatra's Pearls'.

Roman Empire.[xi] Cleopatra's love of the strong stuff, however, isn't simply a matter of legend. The discovery of a document in her own writing showed her ordering one of Antony's generals to 'import 5,000 amphorae of wine from Cos each year with no tax payable', concluding with the phrase 'make it happen'.[xii]

Drinking myths, games and temple tipples

To make the most of all this alcohol, Egyptian religion found uses and misuses of drink as part of religious rites, games and festivities. The veritable Glastonbury of these festivals was a centrepiece of wild proportions, celebrating the saving of humanity from the goddess Hathor through a bacchanalia of drunken misdeed, all to please the gods. It first evolved from a mythic tale where humankind was saved from bloody destruction thanks to the liberal application of a red-hued beer.

The festival known as Tekh – or 'the festival of drunkenness' – would honour the mighty Hathor, largely by behaving as she had in the myth, causing mayhem before passing out with drink. The principal aim of this festival was to get so drunk you were not really cognisant of the present, and as such, all-night parties of drinking and music would blend into morning drumming rituals (not that different from a techno night) and games which enabled the drinkers to lose themselves still further. It was said that at this point the goddess Hathor would come among them, thankfully benign. In this drinking game, the more drunk you were the more you could be face to face with the gods.

---

xi Joann Fletcher, 'Wine in Ancient Egypt II', *Immortal Egypt blog*.
xii Joann Fletcher, 'Wine in Ancient Egypt II'.

Hathor's night to forget

In this tale, the sun god Ra concludes (perhaps correctly) that humanity has not shown enough reverence and deserves punishment. He sends his daughter Hathor, goddess of the sky, of women and fertility, agriculture, childbirth, music, dance and drunkenness, to earth to carry out the deed.

Hathor is normally depicted as a benign god in the form of a cow-headed woman or a cow and is associated with gratitude, kindness, alcohol, fertility and love. However, she comes to earth in the form of her alter ego, a great and fearsome god-lioness known as Sekhmet. The lioness Hathor slaughters all humans she comes across and chases the remainder south from Egypt into Nubia. She does this with such bloodlust that the other gods beseech Ra to intervene to save what is left of humanity.

In an attempt to correct his own bad choices, Ra summons vast quantities of red-coloured beer to flood the whole of Upper Egypt. Hathor, in her bloodlust, sees this great red sea as human blood and, still thirsty, drinks the lot until she keels over drunk. The resulting re-transformation of Sekhmet the bloody into Hathor the boozed saved the human race and Hathor was brought safely home northwards into Egypt with the Egyptian people. Her return to Egypt was forever marked by the annual Nile floods which brought a red-coloured flood of iron-sediment-rich waters across the Nile's banks onto farmland, fertilising the soil and giving cause for a great celebratory drinking game.[xiii]

---

xiii Joann Fletcher, 'Wine in Ancient Egypt I'.

The festival would encourage revellers to transgress usual social boundaries for the night, and festival-goers would routinely engage in all sorts of eye-opening activities and give phallic-shaped offerings to honour Hathor as the goddess of love and the drunken, inadvertent and beer-belching sparer of mankind.

The festival developed so much that a temple was built on the Nile Delta in Bubastis, where annual fertility rites and drunken goings-on would coincide with the great flood. As the waters rose upstream, festival-goers would flow to the temple, each boat-full more inebriated than the last. As they passed settlements they would dance, play music and expose themselves to onlookers.[xiv] Temple inscriptions give lingering impressions of this drunken love festival, with one mural accompanied by the lyrics: 'The channels are filled with water anew and the land is flooded with love.'[xv]

The Egyptians also used wine to please the sacred animals of temple cults that emerged, in what was probably not that much of a game for the animal feeders. In the temple town of Fayum, or in Greek the wonderfully titled Crocodopolis, the crocodile god Sobek had a temple cult of loyal followers both human and reptilian. These sacred crocodiles were reared, kept, bred and then mummified at an enormous temple complex on an inland lake in the Delta. Strabo, an Ancient Greek geographer, described first-hand the luxurious life led by these god-crocs, particularly one called Suchus, who would be fed in the all-too-real game of crocodile god feeding (and drinking) by temple priests:

xiv Joann Fletcher, 'Wine in Ancient Egypt I'.
xv Joann Fletcher, 'Wine in Ancient Egypt I'.

> Our host, one of the officials, who was introducing us into the mysteries there, went with us to the lake, carrying from the dinner [. . .] some roasted meat and a pitcher of wine mixed with honey. We found the animal lying on the edge of the lake; and when the priests went up to it, some of them opened its mouth and another put in the cake, and again the meat, and then poured down the honey mixture.[xvi]

Other games and rites involving alcohol in Ancient Egypt remain something of a mystery. Recent studies on an ancient and enigmatic cup from Egypt which found its way to Florida have discovered that it was likely used for alcoholic and psychedelic drinking rituals. The mug is shaped in the form of the god Bes and analysis of residues within it suggests that it was filled with a heady concoction: sesame, grapes, liquorice, pine nuts and two substances known to cause dream-like visions and psychedelic effects, Syrian rue and Egyptian lotus. Further questions remain as to the reasons for the remnants of bodily fluids, including vaginal mucus, breast milk *and* blood, which were also part of this megacocktail. This vessel was evidently part of a ritualistic drinking game of some kind, though its uses remain mysterious, perhaps related to fertility or regeneration.[xvii]

Drinking games or rituals were a standard part of Egyptian deaths as well as life, with wine left in tombs to

---

xvi Strabo, *Geography*, in 'Sobek: Ancient Egyptian Crocodile God in the Greek and Roman Periods', Rhakotis.

xvii Julia Binswanger, 'Ancient Egyptians Drank Psychedelic Concoctions from This 2,000-Year-Old Mug, Study Finds', *Smithsonian Magazine*, 25 November 2024.

keep the party going long after the last mourners had departed. In the famous tomb of Tutankhamun an entire wine cellar was discovered, along with additional wine jars in the king's main burial chamber (for convenience), one holding red wine and the other white. In fact, the entire tomb complex of the prematurely dead king was only found in its more secluded part of the Valley of the Kings thanks to the uncleanliness of the king's drunken wake-goers. The finding of a discarded alabaster wine goblet inscribed with the king's name led Howard Carter's team to discover the tomb's exact location. It was a common custom for Egyptians to have a noisy annual party above the tomb in which the soul of the deceased would partake.[xviii]

Three thousand years was a lot of time to invent, distil and perfect a range of alcohol and a bizarre array of methods to drink it, from drunken temple antics taking revellers close to the gods in games of drinking to incoherence, to complex and mysterious ritual cocktails of alcohol and all manner of other fluids, to the refined yet outrageous drinking of Egypt's most famous rulers (and crocodiles!). Ancient Egypt's fascinating history most certainly doesn't stop with the mummies, and indeed even they got to enjoy alcohol in and beyond life, as tombs were furnished with stocks of wine and murals to conjure further, everlasting stocks and drinking scenes long after the physical good stuff had been slurped up by the not-so-deceased – but very parched – inside their tomb.

To replicate such a range of drinking games and rituals today could require a lot of specialised equipment, for

xviii Joann Fletcher, 'Wine in Ancient Egypt I'.

example a vast temple complex and associated brewery or, say, a sacred crocodile. Nonetheless, with some small substitutions, there is very little to stop you and whatever motley and unwise collection of associates you can muster from drinking like an Egyptian.

How to drink like an Egyptian

Number of players: However many devotees to Hathor you can find.

You will need:
- A reddish-hued, bread-based, hop-free beer – ideally light and perhaps fruity, to follow the date and pomegranate flavourings used by the Egyptians to mask the bready taste.
- A Levantine wine variety, say from Cyprus, Egypt or Lebanon.
- For the ancient and mysterious spirit, you can really substitute what you like as no one knows for sure what it was made of.
- A crocodile, or substitute.
- A temple substitute or at least assorted Egyptian-style decor.
- A collection of revellers prepared to go the extra mile.
- Honey and other edible treats, such as dates for accuracy.

How to recreate the festival of drunkenness:
1. At a time of renewal in nature, perhaps spring or summer or the coming of the rains, gather a great group of

revellers to put on a feast of drunkenness over at least two days.
2. On the first day, gather revellers to drink, eat and dance their way through the day, allowing them to engage in unruly acts and break cultural norms.
3. Keep them going with more alcohol through the night until at dawn, when they seek sleep, you pound the room with a near hypnotising rhythmic drumming and encourage participants to dance and drink again, with renewed urgency.
4. This cocktail of dance, drink, liberation and drums should deliver a trance-like quality and revellers reportedly should begin to notice the goddess Hathor dancing among them. Though this cannot be guaranteed. If seen, she should be thanked for sparing humanity through a bit too much beer.

How to drink like a sacred crocodile:
1. Designate a willing human or humans to take the part of the sacred crocodiles in the temple of Crocodopolis.
2. In a worshipful manner, all others should attend to the crocodiles, performing libations and drinking while feeding them the finest wine mixed with honey.
3. The author would not recommend mummification of anyone/thing as part of any crocodile-based drinking game.

How to create a wild and wacky cocktail as part of a Hathorian/Dionysian cult:
1. In a suitable vessel, ideally one shaped like the head of an Ancient Egyptian or Greek god of drinking, mix alcohol with suitable (legal and edible) liquids representing a

theme of your choice, perhaps renewal, gratitude or celebration.
2. From this point onwards you and your cult can really design things as you see fit as we have little to no information on how the cocktail cups of Bes were used.

> **Top tip:** Egyptian beer didn't travel well but, to remedy this, great breweries were constructed near sites of ritual. Don't bother bringing a bottle from home, there is always plenty on tap at the temple of Hathor. Don't break any social norms I wouldn't break!

Drinking in America

*Finding Booze in the New World and
Under the Ban, 1600–1950 CE*

Drinking in America is a conundrum and a well-founded one: a rich history of boozy experimentation, a democratisation of European tipples for the masses, the invention of cocktails no less, and yet at the same time America retains a deep concern about youth drinking culture, has a strong tradition of temperance preaching and, most significantly, undertook thirteen years of nationwide Prohibition.

No wonder, then, that America has stories to tell when it comes to drinking games, but to save you, dear reader, from the ignominy and horror of modern American fraternity culture and the depraved and frankly unimaginative goings-on among America's most privileged youth, this chapter will focus on America's foundation to the end of Prohibition and the story of America's drinking and the games that accompanied it.

We find drunken energies engaged in the unusual game of 'How on earth shall we make something to drink here?' played unwillingly by early settlers, and the origin of the now ubiquitous 'beer pong' at Dartmouth College in the 1950s; or the lively games of shot poker, blackjack, dance marathons and liar's dice played in the speakeasies and private saloons of Prohibition. America across this period of time is complicated, inventive, confounded by the desire to build anew but hampered by the cultural baggage of the Old World and fuelled, darkly, by the labour engine of chattel slavery and the conquest and extermination of America's First Nations as the young nation expanded west in its 'pioneering spirit'. The drinking story, too, is complex and entangled by these paradoxes, from the early sale of alcohol to tribes, which still casts a long shadow on reservations today, to the popularisation of rum, a by-product of sugar grown by enslaved Africans across the USA.

A pot-still history of early America

By the mid-seventeenth century, Britain, after a good deal of inter-imperial squabbles and land trading with the French, Dutch and Spanish, had cobbled together thirteen colonies on the east coast of North America. Jamestown, established by the British Virginia Company in 1607, was the first of these, but it and the other colonies endured a rocky start, facing starvation, disease and warfare with the local First Nation peoples whose land they were usurping. Over time, Jamestown was buttressed with more men, supplies and livestock and took up tobacco cultivation, which is recorded as 'highly profitable' in most histories – no doubt due to the less often mentioned labour force of enslaved Africans which from 1619 was growing the cash crop for the colony.[i]

Separately, a group of independent-minded folk and religious non-conformists (except when it came to conforming to naming towns), had sailed from Plymouth to found ... Plymouth, Massachusetts. Further north, Dutch forced purchases of land from the local Delaware, Algonquin, Lenape and Munsee peoples created a little town called 'New Amsterdam', which was becoming a thriving seaport. The English took it over through a show of force in 1664 without a shot being fired and renamed it New York.

From the mid-1650s these colonies grew and prospered, but they were closely bound by the rules imposed upon them by the Crown back in Britain, which ensured that only goods landed (and taxed) first in Britain could flow to America. To an independent-minded group of pioneers intent on forging a new and different path from the Old World, these rules were increasingly unwelcome.

Add to this the re-incorporation of these independent colonies into 'Royal provinces' under George I, wars with both the French and the Native American peoples and the announcement in 1764 that Britain would fund its military forces through taxing in America, and a course was set for independence. The 'stamp' tax on sugar and molasses used

---

i National Park Service, 'Tobacco: Colonial Cultivation Methods', *NPS.gov*.

to fund this military drive was loathed and caused protests across the colonies. These protests grew to openly reject the law across the colonies, and tax collectors and their hated 'stamps' were driven from office, their stamps destroyed, and the act was repealed.

Learning little, the British tried again in 1767 to fill their coffers from American pockets with duties on lead, glass, paper and, most famously, tea. This time riots returned with a vengeance, and dissatisfaction didn't go away. In 1775, in the face of the increasing privations by the Crown, the colonies declared independence within the British Empire, followed in 1776 with a declaration of complete independence.

Following independence, the American union of states grew and developed, expanding with land purchases, deals and steals from colonial powers and original occupiers. In the South, slavery and then deeply unequal segregation produced cotton and tobacco and other goods for free Americans to buy, while resource extraction from the expanding western frontier and the farms of the Midwest produced materials for the industrialising North-East. By the late-nineteenth century, America opened its borders to the huddled masses of the Old World, an action which would come to define the popular image of America for years to come but which masked the oppressed masses of its own.

Yet even the most potent symbol of American independence has links to its drinking, and an Old-World heritage which the fledgling nation couldn't quite let go of. The soundtrack to American statehood, 'The Star-Spangled Banner', is in fact set to the melody of a popular eighteenth-century drinking song called 'To Anacreon in Heaven', which originated in a London gentlemen's club known for wine-sodden musical evenings. And thus the near-sacred icon of American statehood in fact began life as a merry tune which echoed through boozy English banquets.[ii]

The spirit(s) of a fledgling nation

Within this history flows a thread, an actor or catalyst interwoven in the story of America: alcohol. Much like the narrative of America's emergence, its drinking history has been shaped along familiar folds: those of self-made (home-brewed), democratising luxury for all (or perhaps more accurately for most), and of breaking out of Old-World fustiness (adding more than gin to tonic).

With the early pilgrims, their make-do-and-mend attitude was certainly applied to their desperate efforts to produce something drinkable on the tiny eastern edge of the vast and wild North American continent they clung on to. In fact, it was clearly a necessity, though not one the first settlers at Jamestown had anticipated, having forgotten to bring a brewer among their first landing group. The colony had to swiftly advertise for one to join them from Britain in 1609.[iii] Even with a brewer, however, early settlers had trouble translating old techniques to the plants available to them in the New World. Barley grew poorly, but blissfully the apple grew in plentiful supply and with it they made

---

[ii] BBC News, 'The Surprising British Origins of the US National Anthem', *BBC*, 15 April 2024.
[iii] Steven Grasse, *Colonial Spirits: A Toast to Our Drunken History* (New York: Abrams Image, 2016), p. 19.

cider. By independence, nine in ten New England farms made cider and cider vinegar.[iv]

With perseverance they did find something that could get them sozzled effectively, with one colonist writing back that they had found a 'waie to make som good drink of Indian corne',[v] essentially birthing bourbon whiskey. Settlers also found that while barley failed to take, Irish rye wheat did well in the new soils and this led eventually to the development of both rye and bourbon whiskeys.

Before the advent of American whiskey, however, another spirit, darker in appearance and origin, was to dominate America: rum. Rum originated in Barbados, and was known as 'kill-devil' then rumbullion and finally rum, though Brazilian techniques had earlier distilled a different spirit from sugar.[vi] Rum's advantages for scrupulous slave plantation owners were notable, given it was made from the by-products of the sugar industry, a thick waste molasses left to ferment and cut with water, and if you were lucky spices, to produce a raw and potent spirit that took fledgling America by storm.

It was rumoured to cure ailments as diverse as scurvy, malaria, childhood diseases and syphilis,[vii] and quickly became the drink of the colonial period in rum punch and the forerunner to the cocktail the 'sling'. The sling, essentially citrus or another flavouring with rum, sugar and crushed ice, was a southern drink which fell out of

---

iv Steven Grasse, *Colonial Spirits*, p. 45.
v Steen Grasse, *Colonial Spirits*, p. 183.
vi Andrew Barr, *Drink: A Social History of America* (New York: Carroll & Graf Publishers, 1999), p. 34.
vii Steven Grasse, *Colonial Spirits*, p. 92.

popularity, as did the mint julep (a mint sling), today drunk famously at the Kentucky Derby in a revivalist gesture of southern tradition.[viii] Rum was also quickly purported as a medicine against a scourge facing colonial cities each summer, when reportedly hundreds were falling ill and dying of the shock of drinking cold water in the heat. Concern was such that leaflets were printed recommending water to be cut with liquor, usually rum, to avoid the malady, which in fact was likely caused by parasites and bacteria infecting water in the summer heat.

Modern tastes

With the development of the colonies into a nation, new drinking trends and tastes were fast taking shape, but a perennial issue persisted: Americans could not, despite their very best efforts, grow wine. Despite Jefferson's notes, which show his belief that the United States could 'make as great a variety of wines as are made in Europe',[ix] efforts continually failed, first in Florida in the sixteenth century and it was not until the 1800s that any grapes were harvested in the United States.

This failure to grow at home, however, did not prevent Americans from getting their taste of the fair tipple, most notably through the peculiar tale of Madeira wine. Old Madeira wine was popular to trade with the American colonies as it was shipped from a lonely Atlantic island already partway en route to the Americas, which lengthened its

---

viii Andrew Barr, *Drink: A Social History of America*, p. 46.
ix Steven Grasse, *Colonial Spirits*, p. 69.

shelf life. It was also duty free, thanks to a trade alliance between Portugal and Britain.

For a period, however, turbulence in winds and currents around the island, which sits out into the Atlantic some 500 nautical miles south-west of Lisbon, meant ships could not stop there. To maintain their stock, islanders preserved their fresh wine, professionally spoiling it by adding grape spirits and cooking it to create a fortified wine. It was found that this could keep far longer and that the flavour improved as it was rolled in barrels in the humid bowls of ships bound for the New World, a journey that would often spoil unfortified wine. In fact, Madeira was improved so much by this process that later European shipments were often routed via America, with the wine acting as ship's ballast in order to give the same quality and flavour improvements to Europe as were enjoyed in the colonies.

Madeira was immensely popular among the more wealthy of early Americans, so much so that Jefferson toasted independence with it. After independence, French wine too flowed to America, with French estates eager to replace the now headless aristocratic market in post-revolutionary France. The conditions for shipment, however, were still unfavourable and unfortified European wine continued to be a costly luxury for the very richest for years to come.

Beer was initially tricky for early settlers to produce and experimentation was rife to find a way to quench the thirst. So much so that desperate recipes for 'spruce beer' made with pine needles were recorded as a testament to valiant efforts to scratch the itch for a good pint.[x] Though later

---

x Steven Grasse, *Colonial Spirits*, p.25.

ale-style beers were developed in early America, it was only in the industrialising America of the 1800s that beer, today America's tipple of choice in all fifty states, began its rise as the drink of the working man in the saloons that emerged in the cities of the north. Positioned near factories and in town centres, these refectories served beer, cooked lunches and distraction to working-class men. It is often said that women never frequented saloons, but in fact it was common for women to enter to purchase a 'growler' of beer to drink at home, while some women worked in saloons behind the bar or in some cases as sex workers.

Saloons served beer, and a beer quite distinct from the early British-style ales due to two very important factors: the emergence of refrigeration and the influence of German and Czech immigration, which gave America its third independence (from British ale) in the form of Pilsner lager beer. For many years, beer producers in America faced a problem: beer could only be mass-cooled when there was ice (in winter and in northern states), yet beer was most wanted in the South and in summer, where and when it was hot. Brewers had to brew through the winter, estimating what would be drunk the following summer, and would lose money if they fell short of demand or overshot and produced too much which would be wasted. The proliferation of refrigeration, first through specially designed ice houses, ice preservation methods and later actual refrigeration machines, allowed beer to be brewed year-round across the nation by the end of the nineteenth century to quench the thirst of working men and women.[xi] At the same time German emigrant John

---

xi Andrew Barr, *Drink: A Social History of America*, pp. 57, 65.

Wagner was busy brewing a German lager in 1840, having brought with him some German lager yeast on his voyage; this method, combined with Czech immigrants' bright gold Pils-style beer, took off and eventually dominated American beer production, marking true independence from Britain some hundred years after the first declaration.[xii]

At the same time, for the more well-to-do, the punch bowl and mixed rum drink was going from strength to literal strength, slings being increasingly mixed with bitters to make what was called a 'cocktail'. In 1862 the first recorded mention by bartender Jerry Thomas in his guide to mixed drinks described the cocktail as being commonly mixed and bottled for trips to the country, but earlier references show the sling plus bitters being mixed in New York as early as 1806.

The ban and what it brought

All this drinking, however, got a lot of people concerned and a powerful temperance movement emerged in the late nineteenth century. Temperance, in recognition of the impact of the saloon and alcohol misuse by men upon their families, was closely linked with the movement for women's suffrage. Its methods were mixed, from individual renegades like Carry Nation smashing up saloon stocks in their local towns, to marches, speeches and political action with increasing success as some states, like Maine in 1851, became early adopters of prohibition.

xii Andrew Barr, *Drink: A Social History of America*, p. 63.

However, the lack of advertising standards in nineteenth-century America meant it wasn't always easy to avoid the bottle. One historian found that in the early 1900s a journalist surveyed members of the Women's Christian Temperance Union and discovered that 75 per cent of its members consumed health tonics that were in fact strongly alcoholic despite the protestations of their labels; these included Parker's Tonic, 'purely vegetable' and 'for inebriates', which was 42 per cent ABV, Hoofland's German Bitters, 'free from alcoholic stimulant' but in fact 26 per cent alcohol, and Colden's Liquid Beef Tonic, which was 'recommended for the treatment of alcohol habit' and no doubt well received at 27 per cent alcohol.[xiii]

Despite such teething problems, the temperance movement grew and grew and, with concerted effort, brought about National Prohibition under the Eighteenth Amendment in 1920. Political concern regarding the impact of widespread alcoholism on health, on morality, on crime and on the family concluded that only drastic action would do. Under the 'Volstead Act' it was illegal for any American to buy, sell or consume alcohol, though loose drafting in Section 29 allowed persons to make 'non intoxicating fruit juices' for their own consumption, a bracket that was used increasingly liberally in the years following the ban. Prohibition was in force during the First World War but it was in 1920 that the ban was fully enforced and a truly national endeavour. On the night before Prohibition, a great rift could be felt across America with many celebrating while others mourned. At the Golden Glades restaurant (and ice rink) in New York, an open coffin circled the dance

---

xiii Andrew Barr, *Drink: A Social History of America*, p,135.

floor as the 'last glass' of each attendee was thrown ceremonially into the casket.[xiv]

A most resourceful nation

Americans, ever resourceful, quickly found means of making and getting hold of something to keep their spirits up. Bootlegging, the art of making your own supply, was for some an easy return to earlier days of self-reliance. For corn spirit distillers in the back country, the making of 'moonshine' (illicit spirit from distilled corn) exploded with greater demand for it on the black market but also higher overheads as one had to pay off whoever knew about one's nefarious brewing. Americans are estimated to have produced 700 million gallons of beer at home in the Prohibition period,[xv] with half a million actively employed in the illicit trade by the mid twenties.[xvi] Some made it themselves while others spread the risk, like Frankie Yale, a Brooklyn mobster who paid families $15 a day to run a still in their kitchens.[xvii]

Drink was also smuggled in to the US, with Canadian whiskey firm Seagram doing so flagrantly well out of Prohibition that it paid the US government $1.5 million in a negotiated settlement after Prohibition was over.[xviii] Other

[xiv] Eric Burns, *The Spirits of America: A Social History of Alcohol* (Philadelphia: Temple University Press, 2004), p. 189.
[xv] Eric Burns, *The Spirits of America*, p. 190.
[xvi] Eric Burns, *The Spirits of America*, p. 203.
[xvii] W. J. Rorabaugh, *Prohibition: A Very Short Introduction* (Oxford: Oxford University Press, 2020), p. 69.
[xviii] Andrew Barr, *Drink: A Social History of America*, p. 193.

tell-tale signs of this smuggling trade can be seen in export figures, with Moët & Chandon exports to Canada rising from 1,000 cases to 22,000 in 1923, only to fall back after Prohibition.[xix]

Where to party?

As well as making their own, Americans also found new ways to drink with others, from the party at home to the speakeasy secret bars that abounded, at least for those with the right connections and, predictably, the right kind of income. In 1929 the police commissioner of New York City estimated there to be 32,000 such establishments in the city, twice as many as the legal establishments which were licensed before Prohibition. Mostly speakeasies had wealthy patrons, with the best jazz music, high-end chefs and the rest, but to keep the police off the scent by deterring too many patrons, the price of entry and drinks was marked up between two and ten times what one might otherwise have paid. Disguises also helped, with one notably inventive undertaker's in Detroit discovered to be bringing in coffin-fulls of illicit booze for the mourners gathering in its parlours.[xx] While Prohibition left legacies like the now-celebrated institution the Stork Club, which began life as a New York speakeasy, it also left a trail of shame. It's suspected that untold tens of thousands died of alcohol poisoning from wood alcohol or moonshine or other illicit bootlegs in the period.

xix Andrew Barr, *Drink: A Social History of America*, p. 133.
xx Eric Burns, *The Spirits of America*, p. 200.

A big winner of Prohibition was the cocktail; this way to hide the taste of bootlegged spirits developed into a skilled and fashionable trend. The lack of quality alcohol for most did, however, lead to some quite unusual and perhaps unrepeatable inventions during Prohibition, for example the 'Yack Yack Bourbon' in Chicago, mainly comprised of raw alcohol with iodine for flavour, or the sadly (or not) forgotten alcoholic milkshake. Some mixologists did find hits, developing some of the now classics including the Gin Alexander (gin, crème of cacao and cream), the Jack Rose (apple brandy, grenadine and citrus juice) and thanks to the availability of gin, the Martini, which would go on to become the status symbol of middle-class America, with Franklin D. Roosevelt mixing the first legal Martini just moments after the repeal of Prohibition in 1933.

Prohibition in posterity; grandfather of college drinking games

After that first Martini was legally mixed by the commander-in-chief, the results of Prohibition could really be seen. It left a long shadow in more socially conservative states, with Mississippi only repealing Prohibition in 1966 and over 100 state counties remaining 'dry' (banning the sale of alcohol) to this day. Beyond this, the ban totally changed the social and cultural norms of America.

After Prohibition, going to bars was no longer a male preserve: women drank at speakeasies and parties as they never had pre-Prohibition. With this change came an improvement (though marginal) in women's independence and cultural expectations around their behaviour. It became daring, yes, but not unthinkable to be dancing with men, and even kissing before marriage was increasingly seen, if often berated. Cocktails and gregarious dancing became commonplace in more liberal America and among the more wealthy of its occupants, and it was in these cocktail-fuelled speakeasies, parties and dances that Americans played the drinking games of Prohibition.

> Both sellers and buyers found ways to get around the ban with some very inventive methods. In the Napa Valley, an expected casualty of Prohibition, some vineyards in California's wine region increased production through the sale of 'raisin cakes'. These cakes (clumps of dried raisins), allowed under the act for the production of fruit juices at home, were sold by wholesalers who employed women to demonstrate and warn against the wine-making properties of these cakes with stern faces, cautioning buyers not to place the cake in a jug with water for twenty-one days then bottle with a cork or wine could be created; in fact, the cakes' packaging explicitly warned buyers that they could 'ferment and turn into wine'. Buyers would feign concern and note the need to avoid inadvertently and carelessly leaving the raisin cakes in water for twenty-one days before bottling and accidentally producing wine rather than the juice they so clearly desired.[xxi]

xxi Edward Behr, *Prohibition: The Thirteen Years That Changed America* (New York: Arcade Publishing, 1997), p. 91.

For students, middle-class Americans and the much-famed 'flappers' of the 1920s and early '30s, defying the law and the social expectations of their elders was a game in itself. Yet once out and on the illicit scene, games abounded both in speakeasies and in the act of getting hold of the stuff.

Dances like the foxtrot or the less glamorous sounding 'turkey trot' emerged where men and women could dance together, and dance marathons were a common pastime both in and outside of illicit drinking establishments. Rumoured games of speakeasies would see roulette wheel gambling, with the loser drinking up, or blackjack, played in a similar vein. Cards were common enough that authorities in New York opened a honey (or gin) trap as a speakeasy called the 'Bridge Whist Club' in 1925 to catch out bar-goers.

Some suggest the origins of the 'game' (or social torture tool) of 'never have I ever' are rooted in this era of newfound liberation where men and women could mix unchaperoned. Other fragments of games played in this era exist but the precise details are hard to define. One example is the 1920s board game of 'On Me!' in which players used a counter styled as their favourite cocktail and likely faced a strong measure of drinking forfeits, though surviving details are scant.

As the repeal of Prohibition passed, the upheaval in societal expectations it created only accelerated drinking game culture. Boosted by the societal changes of the Second World War, by the 1950s (some) women and men, rich white ones at least, were interacting at colleges and revelling in the fruits of liberalising culture brought about in part through Prohibition. In any case, it was in this era and the decades which followed that many of the drinking games we know today were forged, with beer pong allegedly invented in Dartmouth College in the 1950s as pingpong was interrupted by cups left on a table-court. It first used paddles to propel the balls towards an opponent's cups but by 1979 it's evident that fraternities at Lehigh University, Pennsylvania, decided to dispose of paddles entirely and use their hands to throw the balls instead. Today there is, rather alarmingly, a beer pong world series with over 500 teams.

How to play drinking games of the speakeasies

With wine-making raisin cakes hard to find and the rules of later drinking games well trodden, we'll focus our attention on the drinking games of the speakeasies. All manner of twenties-style paraphernalia exists to kit out your attempt to drink like a flapper, so go wild for the glitz and the glamour and wear strong shoes for a twenty-four-hour turkey trot!

You will need:
- A suitably discreet and exclusive venue akin to a speakeasy.
- Gin, rum, poor-quality whiskey, lemon, sugar syrup, bitters and fruit juices, plus ice (the cocktail kit of the 1920s).
- Decks of cards.
- A spinning roulette wheel.
- A dance floor.
- 1920s music or if you have means or talented friends, musicians.

- A host of excited guests liberated from the social mores of their era through the thrill of lawbreaking.
- Dance guides or online tutorials for the top dances of the 1920s.

How to play shot poker and shot blackjack:
1. When playing these two classic card games, which need little introduction, try to fashion your game in the spirit of an underground speakeasy, hidden and exclusive but luckily for you no longer reliant on bootleg alcohol or the need to dodge police to the door.
2. Get your glamorous associates a drink, a classic Prohibition-era cocktail, of course, and settle down round the green felt for some classic speakeasy-style gaming.
3. For every 'bust' in poker or blackjack (also known as 21 or pontoon) take a drink (responsibly!) until the game is won, lost or abandoned.

How to play a dance marathon drinking game:
1. Follow some online tutorials or dance step guides for the foxtrot, turkey trot, the lindy hop or the charleston.
2. Find a willing partner and get to work, adding your newly learned steps to classic jazz tracks of the Prohibition dance floors. Try:
    - 'Ain't Misbehavin'' by Fats Waller
    - 'Sweet Georgia Brown' by Ben Bernie & His Hotel Roosevelt Orchestra
    - Or the just post-Prohibition but epic 'Minnie the Moocher' by Cab Calloway
3. For every break in dancing take a forfeit drink, though do remember to hydrate (with water) along the way; dancers need not be penalised for water breaks.

Top tip: for a more pleasurable experience ensure you use cocktail mixers and fruit juices to mask and dilute the 'bootleg' alcohol of the Prohibition era. This is essential for a night to remember as during the period industrial alcohol was used to illicitly produce imitation spirits with sometimes disastrous consequences.

Highlands, High Duties, High Jinks

Scotland, Alcohol and the Union, circa 1600–1850

It is sometimes said, smugly, that *in whisky, Scotland is distilled*, and no doubt the whisky bore who tells you this will leave pause for you to dwell on their frankly silly statement. During this pause you can reflect that while this vision of the simple purity of Scottish culture, reflected in an expensive (and delicious) amber spirit, is attractive, it masks a truer, more real and human vision of Scottish drinking history. One we can read through a murky mess of claret, of illicit Highland stills, smuggling, anti-English drinking clubs and boisterous drinking games like high jinks.

Indeed, Scotland's world-renowned and malty export, steeped in tradition, complexity and implied exclusivity, is far from the only way to take a slightly unsteady jaunt through Scottish history. In fact, it's believed that the origin of distilling in Scotland, and perhaps Europe, was the development of stills to strengthen mead rather than malt as early as the sixth century.[i] Ever since then, and probably before, Scotland's had a lively history surrounding alcohol: from the taste for French wines as a deliberate affront to integration with England, to the resistance of remote whisky distillers, to the advances of the British tax authorities or the extensive range of drinking establishments which proliferated in Scotland's cities as they industrialised.

In any case, the ingenuity of Scotland's inhabitants to make fun with very limited materials (think shepherds knocking stones about to create golf or chilly fishermen sliding rocks across an icy loch to invent curling), has naturally tended to lean on its tipples to keep the chilly nights alive. Scotland's bard Robert Burns writes of unusual drinking games among Scottish gentlemen involving good wines and an ebony whistle, while the old Scottish drinking game of 'high jinks' (the origin of the term), involving dice, wild unruliness and strong drinking forfeits, is recorded by Sir Walter Scott and others.

---

i Gina Hames, *Alcohol in World History* (London: Routledge, 2012), p. 41.

HIGHLANDS, HIGH DUTIES, HIGH JINKS

Scotland's history in a glass

The slice of Scottish history from 1600 to 1850 covers a transformational period in the fortunes and alliances of the nation. During this time it transitioned from an independent kingdom allied with France against the hated English to a part of the Union of Great Britain *with* the hated English. Though it may have dissolved its ancient parliament, under the union Scotland kept many of its understandable grievances against its neighbour whom Burns decried as a 'parcel of rogues in a nation'.

After decades of religious, political and battlefield differences, Scotland and England were brought abruptly side by side in 1603 after the death of the heirless Queen Elizabeth I of England. Her death and lack of children meant the English crown fell to the then king of Scotland, James (VI in Scotland becoming James I in England – keep up!), under the union of the two crowns. Far from a happy marriage, this state of affairs did foster an ever-growing alignment of the two kingdoms. However, this was not without hiccups, including the Gunpowder Plot in 1605, where Catholic plotting sought to blow up an English parliament about to vote for greater union between Scotland and England which they feared would lead to Catholic persecution. With the plot defeated, efforts to align would culminate in 1707 in the Union of England and Scotland in the Kingdom of Great Britain.

1707 was far from the end of enmity between England and Scotland, as any sporting match contested between the two today can still demonstrate. Indeed, well before 1707 a rump of discontent in Scotland against the ever-closer union with England brewed to a furore when King James was ousted by William of Orange in 1688. His supporters, the Jacobites, kept the flame alive and continued to fight bloodily for Scottish freedom and the return of their king over the water in the Jacobite risings from 1689 to 1746. The final phase of this bloody period of Scottish uprising and English repression reared its head in 1745 when James's grandson, known as 'Bonnie Prince Charlie', arrived in Scotland and raised an army to fight the English and reclaim the Scottish throne. This ragtag band of freedom fighters was repressed without mercy at the Battle of Culloden in 1746, where English troops routed Prince Charlie's troops in what would to date be the last land battle on British soil.

From then on Scotland remained a proud, independent-minded and grudge-keeping partner in the Union of Great Britain, earning its keep as a fundamental part of Britain's imperially fuelled Industrial Revolution. Glasgow's western-facing port became a centre of dubious mercantilism, with industrialists growing rich from trade with British possessions in the Caribbean, trading in enslaved Africans and the produce of plantations they were forced to work on. Meanwhile, in Edinburgh a 'Scottish Enlightenment' was developing as thinkers and scientists, novelists, poets and painters wrought a Scottish canon in the image of the nation's (sometimes imagined) past, just as the very present they found themselves in was changing rapidly.

By the mid-nineteenth century, Scotland had grown into an industrial powerhouse of the British Empire, with mining, shipbuilding and distilling, along with cruel investments in the colonies, driving rapid societal change at home. Across this period Scotland's ways of life changed markedly as new technologies, laws and mass movement transformed traditional ways of life, particularly in the

Highlands, where landowners cleared ancient communities from their roots and their movement south drove people to find work in the growing workshop of the central belt. On one hand prosperity for a lucky few generated its own Scottish Enlightenment of arts, philosophy and science, while on the other working conditions for the labouring classes developed social movements in non-conformist churches and unionism that would set out political and religious trends that remain grounded in Scotland today.

All this social change brought with it great changes in how Scotland drank, moving, as we'll see, from an old predilection for the French claret to find whisky, a lonely employer in the depopulated Highlands, as the (strictly commercially speaking) perfect spirit to market to its early industrialising towns, with or without the taxman's consent.

An 'up yours' predilection for claret

While whisky might be planted in the image of Scottish drinking habits, historian Charles Ludington has uncovered an unusual story of a Scottish love of 'claret', a relatively young red wine from the regions of Gascony and Bordeaux, around the period of unionisation. An enduring love of the red stuff north of the border, long after it was officially banned under strict trade embargoes in the rest of Britain, was driven in part by a taste for the products of the old Kingdom of Scotland's 'Auld Alliance' with France, and partly as a signal to the hated English. Its popularity even while Britain (including Scotland) was actively at war with France is a liquid demonstration of Scottish respect for the Union; we might be together in one state but Scotland's taste matches its character: independent, full-bodied and the antithesis of Englishness. Scotland had enjoyed red Bordeaux since the thirteenth century and saw no reason to be moved from its love of the *grand cru* as a result of English laws.

To keep claret flowing into Scotland after the Act of Union in 1707, huge efforts were made to smuggle great quantities of the stuff through Scottish ports, lochs, inlets and beaches. Its presence across Scotland was ubiquitous and confounded English soldiers sent north to 'pacify' the Highlands in 1725, one of whom wrote (as part of a snobbish put-down of Scottish hospitality):

> We have one great advantage that makes amends for many inconveniences. That is the wholesome and agreeable drink, I mean French Claret which is to be had almost anywhere in public houses of any note except in the heart of the highlands and sometimes even there.[ii]

Just as the soldiers were confounded by claret's availability in Scotland, compared to its rarity in England, where war with France and a long-standing alliance with Portugal meant wine predominately was Portuguese or Spanish, customs officials in London were driven to their wits' end attempting to stem the deep red tide that continued to flow. Scottish officials, who in some cases appear to have willingly ignored illegal shipments, were often blamed, and the more efforts from the south were stepped up to halt the trade, the greater the anti-English sentiment that drove much of the demand for claret became.

[ii] Charles C. Ludington, '"To the King O'er the Water": Scotland and Claret, c. 1660–1763', in *A Social and Cultural History of Alcohol*, ed. by Mack B. Holt (Oxford: Berg, 2006), p. 170.

Scottish ingenuity was stretched to breaking point by the range of methods taken up to give the people their claret; smuggling efforts were affectionately known as 'fair trading' and considered a most respectable crime.[iii] Nonetheless, these efforts were often brazen and sometimes downright reckless, ranging from labelling fraud to port of origin changes, to night-time unloading or even the deliberate wrecking of old ships 'bound for Norway' with huge cargoes of claret that could be unloaded from the stricken vessels as 'salvage' without duty or prosecution. Some efforts barely concealed their contents from officials, with the customs records for the Edinburgh port of Leith in 1745 showing huge numbers of 'Portuguese wines' being landed in hogshead casks. For those not in the know, hogshead casks of this type — what we might know as the classic size barrel today — were made exclusively in Southwest France and used, you guessed it, to store and age claret.[iv]

All this claret had to go somewhere, and in the period around and after the Acts of Union more often than not it was drunk as a deliberate 'up yours' to the English in a nostalgic nod to the old Kingdom of Scotland and its heroes. Drinking to this romanticised and proud past was such a popular pastime that special drinking groups (made up of ordinary men only) were set up especially for the purpose of demeaning their southerly Union partner. These Jacobite clubs in Edinburgh included the Auld Scots, the No Surrender, the National, the Anti-English, the Auld

---

iii Ludington, '"To the King O'er the Water": Scotland and Claret, c. 1660–1763', p. 173.
iv Ludington, '"To the King O'er the Water": Scotland and Claret, c. 1660–1763' pp. 172–4.

Reekie and the Scotia's Pride. These groups would meet in 'howffs', a type of Scottish tavern which served claret and basic food, where they would sing, drink down the claret of their old ally and toast to the king over the water (a reference to the banished House of Stuart of which 'Bonnie Prince Charlie' was a member) and the 'cassin o the wanchancie covenant', Scots for 'the repeal of this unlucky union'.[v]

O thou, my muse! guid auld Scotch drink! (Burns)

Whisky, from the Gaelic for water of life, *uisge beatha* or *usquebaugh* – or Aquae vitae in Latin – as it is first recorded, or John Barleycorn as Robert Burns affectionately called it, has a rich story in Scottish history, a story that, remarkably, goes hand in hand (or head to head for a good part of it) with tax, and not only as a stiffener for the nerves when the brown letter drops.

Scottish whisky, which is always made of just three ingredients – cereals, water and yeasts – must be matured for at least three years in oak and be at least 40.0 per cent ABV to earn its title. Single malt whisky must be made from a mash of only malted barley and made at a single distillery using a pot still process. The distinctive taste can come from both the process of the whisky-making, for example if peat is used for the heating of the malted barley with peated fires, or from the storage of the spirit, which might age the stuff

---

[v] Ludington, '"To the King O'er the Water": Scotland and Claret, c. 1660–1763'.

in used sherry casks or charred oak casks from American bourbon production. Casks give the spirit inside them some of the character of their former occupant and give a distinct flavour to the end result.

First recorded in 1494 in the Exchequer Rolls of Scotland (tax records of the day), an entry lists: 'Eight bolls of malt to Friar John Cor wherewith to make aqua vitae,' which according to the Scotch Whisky Association would be enough to make 1,500 bottles of the stuff. From then on, tax and whisky are an unhappy pairing in Scottish history, with a tax later introduced in 1644 which drove whisky producers underground. This tax of 2 shillings and 8 pence was imposed on every Scots pint produced.[vi]

> A Scots pint? I hear you ask. Yes, a Scots pint or a *joug*, made up of course of other Scotch measures, was equivalent to four *mutchkins*, or two *chopins* or sixteen *gills*; and eight Scots pints made a Scottish gallon. True to stereotype, the Scots pint was roughly equivalent to three imperial (standard) pints or around 1.7 litres, and was one of a set of Scottish measuring units in use officially from at least the fifteenth century to 1685, when England's marginally less ridiculous imperial measures were forced upon the Scots. Yet informally these measures, including the Scots pint, were used until the early 1800s, though mainly only in old Scottish bakers' recipes.

---

vi Scotch Whisky Association, 'Story of Scotch', *Scotch-Whisky.org*.

The tax battle for a greater share of whisky's proceeds raged on between Scottish and English tax collectors and politicians until 1823, as successive parliaments in London attempted to extract more tax from what they saw as a wayward Scottish collection system. These wayward taxmen included one Robert Burns, who despite being employed as a duty and excise officer routinely mocked the complex taxation system that evolved unsteadily around whisky in several of his poems.

In the eighteenth century, Scottish whisky was produced initially by small producers in the Highlands, but by the end of the century this was matched by a growing Lowland mass production as industrialisation simplified the process. By 1781 the Lowlands were producing 400,000 gallons a year in large-scale distilleries, while in the Highlands thousands of illicit cottage stills produced untold gallons of the stuff. In just one parish in Argyll, thirty producing stills could be found in the 1780s.[vii] Overall by 1782 some 20,000 stills were in clandestine operation across the Highlands.[viii] Edinburgh, too, had a problem despite the presence of enforcement with eight legal and 400 illegal distilleries in 1779, yet it was those remote areas without any excise official in residence that thrived; on Islay, perhaps the epicentre of modern Scotch, production flourished untaxed and unhindered by regulation.

Policing and taxing this was completely impractical and whisky was so central to Highland life that the task was more or less impossible anyway. Attempts were made at preventing

---

vii Vivien E. Dietz, 'The Politics of Whisky: Scottish Distillers, the Excise, and the Pittite State', *Journal of British Studies*, 36.1 (January 1997), p. 47.

viii Vivien Dietz, 'The Politics of Whisky', p. 50.

exports from Highlands to Lowlands and Scotland to England to protect the value of more taxed products further south but this was countered by smuggling on a vast scale. The demand was causing other problems too. Records from 1790 show the town of Stranraer, with some 1,600 inhabitants, was consuming 24,000 gallons of whisky; elsewhere reports were made of day labourers drinking two chopin bottles (a Scotch measure) of whisky a day from a local shop.[ix] Government concerns around public drunkenness aroused political action and, like the Gin Acts in England, Scotland levied higher taxes but in doing so drove the market for the licit dram sky high, doubling the price it sold for in the Highlands when sold on the black market in Lowland Scotland.

The entire unwieldy, complex and untaxable mass of illicit, remote Scottish distillation was finally brought into legality in 1823 when the Exchequer reduced the spirits duty by half and offered a simple and universal licence to distil to anyone who could pay for it. That same year one George Smith in the secret whisky stronghold of Glenlivet licensed a suspiciously well-established set of stills to formally 'found' the distillery which to this day remains a hallmark of Speyside's most famous produce.

A wild medley of drinking spots

All this toasting, smuggling and distilling created a veritable range of places in which to regale oneself with these ill-gotten drinks and drink Highland whisky by the chopin and French claret by the joug. Scotland developed a range of

---

[ix] Vivien Dietz, 'The Politics of Whisky', p. 63.

establishments to quench the thirst of its inhabitants where drinking games like high jinks were played and the English resoundingly cursed for good measure. Scottish pubs and taverns were a social space which differed from the male-dominated English alehouses; they were a less elitist space where a great mix of workers would drink and debate.

Men still dominated these spaces but it was far from the case that women were isolated from drinking culture as a whole. In addition to taverns and howffs, private drinking houses were commonplace and usually sold beer brewed almost always by women. Women dominated and were often renowned for the brewing of beer from the medieval period until the industrialisation of the process when smaller-scale production became uncompetitive. In a list of the 152 'brewsters' in Aberdeen in 1509, all of them were women. Women could also be taverners (proprietors of taverns) and these taverns grew and grew in popularity. In Dumfries in 1792 there were two inns and forty-nine taverns, while in Victorian Dundee there was one tavern for every twenty-four families.[x]

In addition to the tavern, alehouse, howff, drinking house, pub, dram shop, licenced grocer and tippling house, all of which were common and distinct types of Scottish refectories and drinking establishments, as industrialisation took hold and Irish Catholic communities sought work in Scotland's industries a further type of drinking house, the *shebeen*, came into existence, mainly in Glasgow. These establishments had a (mostly) unfair reputation of operating on the line of the law and were predominantly for Irish communities, usually female owned and run, and

---

x Anthony Cook, *A History of Drinking: The Scottish Pub Since 1700* (Edinburgh University Press, 2015), pp. 3–9.

sometimes (though far from always) doubling as brothels. Shebeens were running at least until the 1930s in Glasgow based on press records, and the name lived on in South Africa where, under apartheid, township lodging and drinking houses were known as shebeens.[xi]

Drinking games of high jinks and whistles

All these drinks and drinking houses garnered a range of drinking games, some more bizarre than others and many no doubt lost to time. Some, however, do remain, if recorded somewhat puzzlingly. The Scottish bard Robert Burns chronicled Scottish drinking in his famous poem 'Tam o'Shanter' but he also wrote verse in celebration of an unusual drinking game he witnessed in the home of the Scottish aristocrat Robert Riddle. Burns watched three Scottish lords drink themselves under the table playing a bizarre drinking game in which essentially the last man to actually be able to blow upon an ebony whistle at the end of the night wins. In Burns's experience the winner apparently drank eight bottles of claret then stood and blew the whistle while his competitors either collapsed in situ or fell to bed. Burns's poem 'The Whistle' commemorates the evening with the opening line remembering 'three joyous good fellows'.

Better recorded still in novels and extracts is the Scots drinking game of High Jinks. 'High jinks' is now a slightly outdated term for mischievous goings-on but it started life (as hey jinks) as the moniker for a lively Scottish drinking game in the seventeenth century. The Scots word 'jink' at

[xi] Anthony Cook, *A History of Drinking: The Scottish Pub Since 1700*, p.14.

that time meant to turn quickly, jerkily or move across to the side or to trick or cheat, while 'high' or 'hoy' comes from an exclamation to encourage action.[xii] Though the origin of the game is disputed (with an early use by Erasmus in 1683, of which more later),[xiii] it's certain that the game if not created in Scotland was played regularly and boisterously there from the 1600s onwards.

The Miriam Webster dictionary links *Hey-Jinks* to a dice game of chance as listed in a 1699 compendium with an explanation simply as: '*Highjinks*: A Play at Dice who Drinks.' Yet wider sources show the game was more complex than this enigmatic description. It appears then that High Jinks was played with dice, drinks and jinks, and with these three simple ingredients a lexical legacy was wrought. Dice would be thrown between two competitors and the loser would complete an agreed action or face a more serious penalty. More often than not this task was a choice between drinking all the contents of the loser's drink vessel (let's hope not a Scots pint!) or undertaking a silly task. It was, of course, the silly task chooser rather than the drinker who gave the modern phrase 'high jinks' its fame.

In Sir Walter Scott's 1815 novel *Guy Mannering*, High Jinks is mentioned as a pastime in some wonderfully phrased detail:

> ... the frolicsome company had begun to practise the ancient and now forgotten pastime of High-jinks.

xii Way With Words, 'High Jinks: Origin and Meaning', waywordradio.org.
xiii Merriam-Webster, 'High Jinks – Meaning and Origin', *Merriam-Webster Dictionary*.

HIGHLANDS, HIGH DUTIES, HIGH JINKS

> This game was played in several different ways. Most frequently the dice were thrown by the company, and those upon whom the lot fell were obliged to assume and maintain, for a time, a certain fictitious character, or to repeat a certain number of fescennine verses in a particular order. If they departed from the characters assigned, or if their memory proved treacherous in the repetition, they incurred forfeits, which were either compounded for by swallowing an additional bumper, or by paying a small sum towards the reckoning. At this sport the jovial company were closely engaged, when Mannering entered the room.[xiv]

'An additional bumper' means another drink, while 'fescennine' is, rather wonderfully, defined as words or verse which are obscene or scurrilous in nature. Scott's description also adds the measure of a challenge to take on a fictitious persona as a means of forfeit as well as a financial charge to the game's loser.

Disappointingly, there are limited alternative sources for High Jinks as a game, as the later use of the term to mean any kind of boisterous or bizarre mischief obscures evidence of the original Scots game. A translation of a text by the Dutch philosopher Erasmus also bizarrely mentions the term 'hey jinks', though Erasmus died in 1536 and the translation in English was made in 1683. The term is unlikely to be a literal translation and the passage doesn't give mention to the game associated with the term, but this shows perhaps that even by the seventeenth century the game's association with the bizarre, the boisterous and the unruly was becoming so synonymous as to take on a literal meaning of its own.

---

xiv Walter Scott, *Guy Mannering* (1815), p. 140.

So we can read Scotland's history in this period in its changing drinking games and customs, from the cursing of the English with jougs of French claret, to the smuggling of Highland whisky past the tax collector's nose or the drinking games of High Jinks and other antics in the plethora of Scottish drinking places it developed in the nineteenth century.

How to high jink like a proud Jacobite

Number of players: As many stout-hearted companions as you can fit in an alehouse, howff, tavern, drinking house, shebeen, inn or other Scottish drinking establishment.

You will need:
- Dice.
- Supplies of good, but not excellent, claret, ideally smuggled.
- A range of Highland small still whiskies (again the more illicit the better).
- A Scots-English dictionary.
- A roaring, but safe, fire.

How to play:
1. In rounds, throw dice competitively, and agree that the total for a set number of rolls will define the score, say the total after three. This will increase the tension.
2. After the rolls, each player has a total and the lowest score loses that round.
3. At this point the game moves to its forfeit stage, where the loser must choose between drinking their glass or undertaking a 'high jink'.

4. If they choose the high jink (which must be silly, lively and bemusing but not so embarrassing as to deter it being chosen) they must then undertake the agreed action immediately.
5. Sir Walter Scott's description of High Jinks includes the forfeit of assuming a fictitious character for the remainder of the game. Players also faced a further forfeit for breaking out of their act. Another forfeit could be issued for failing to recite an agreed lewd and amusing poem or rhyme in the correct order, requiring the player to drink further and recite again. Scott's version also includes a financial opt-out whereby the loser can pay to avoid the required 'high jink' or drink. We recommend this option is ignored.
6. You can, of course, also make up your own type of high jinks. They could include:
    - Faux operatic singing of pop hits
    - Gymnastic feats in the style of animals
    - Practical (but nice) jokes on participating friends
7. These high jinks could be suggested before each round, or a number written out before the game and chosen from a hat.
8. While playing, continue to boisterously raise a glass of claret or a dram of John Barleycorn to the king o'er the water and the cassin o' the wanchancie covenant for good measure.

Top tip: when playing High Jinks, be sure to have a range of bizarre fictitious characters at the ready to ensure forfeits are most difficult for the loser and most entertaining for everyone else.

Libation and Liberation

*Palm Wine and Akpeteshie in
Ghana, circa 1850–1962*

Across the great pre-colonial civilisations of Sub-Saharan Africa, from the Kingdom of Kongo to Great Zimbabwe or the kingdom of Benin in West Africa or the great Empire of Askum in modern-day Ethiopia, many developed their own alcohols, which were a core part of their social and ceremonial worlds.

Ethiopian civilisations developed a special type of honey wine known as '*tedj*', while in lush edges of the Great Rift Valley (modern-day Uganda, eastern Congo and western Kenya and Tanzania) a beer brewed from fermented bananas was created. In Southern Africa beers from millet grains were drunk and in West Africa, palm wine was the beverage of choice. All of these are still drunk in these regions today, alongside European-style beers and spirit imports.

West Africa's liberal use of palm wine, the fresh and delicious fermented sap of the raffia palm, in pre-colonial ritual and social life laces the pages of Nigerian literature, for example Ben Okri's *The Famished Road* or Chinua Achebe's *Things Fall Apart*. In the Ashanti Kingdom, then the Gold Coast and later independent Ghana, palm wine, imported spirts and akpeteshie, a concentrated distillate of palm wine also known as Ogogoro, are at the centre of a complex web of wild drinking rituals and traditions, from libations to gods to the celebrations of births, of coming of age and of deaths. Under colonial rule, palm wine and the rise of drinking akpeteshie was used as a refreshing act of resistance against the British, who banned it, becoming a (literally) strong symbol of the Ghanaian independence movement, the essential accompaniment to the beat of Ghanaian jazz fusion known as 'highlife' which flourished hand in hand with Ghanaian akpeteshie.

It is too much of a stretch (and inconsiderate of their complex roots in traditional beliefs) to call these drinking cultures 'games'. However, the way palm wine and akpeteshie are drunk and their social impact across Ghanaian history is a fascinating story that deserves to be told. So, reader, if you'll permit us we'll take a brief diversion from games to follow the story of akpeteshie, the spirit, if you'll excuse the pun, of Ghanaian independence, from ritual to roaring thirties and refreshment to revolution.

From Ashanti, to Gold Coast, to Ghana

Ghana, like Benin, has the unusual attribute of being named after an ancient kingdom which was not in its modern borders. The Saharan Ghana Empire, which ruled land around the sources of the Niger and Senegal rivers from the seventh to the thirteenth century, would today sit within the borders of Mali and Mauritania in the Sahel. Yet such was the reputation of the ancient empire as a powerful and independent African state, and its mythic connection to the people of modern-day Ghana, that it was chosen in 1957 as a name befitting the new and liberated West African nation.

Modern-day Ghana has within it the roots of many different historic kingdoms and kin-groups; in the north the kingdoms of Bono, Dagomba and Banda had strongholds, while in the south a series of kingdoms known as the Akan States were found. By the early eighteenth century one of these states had created a union of the Akan peoples called the Ashanti Empire, which came to dominate its northern neighbours and directly control its local coastal region to the south.

The empire was a centre of gold production and both royalty and a wealthy class of traders and artisans created and collected gold ornaments and jewellery, also trading them with neighbouring states. Ruled by King Osei Tutu under the symbol of the Golden Stool, the empire took the emblem of a red porcupine as it went from military strength to strength, and the capital of Kumasi became a revered centre of learning, art, architecture and power. Another product of this great empire was that of palm wine, an essential for social events, religious ceremonies and celebratory moments, as well as an indicator of power and wealth.

For the Ashanti elite, alcohol was far from reserved for ritual occasions. Records show that in Kumasi, Ashanti kings and their retinues would regularly set up court in the marketplace to show off. In these marketplace sessions ordinary folk were able to petition the king and court, and a lucky few could even collect and drink the palm wine which missed the king's lips – the gold calabash cup he drank from evidently didn't have the best pour – and fell from his beard into the cups of waiting hangers-on. To drink this beard-drip wine was considered a great honour.

Palm wine is drunk across West Africa, while other versions of the drink are found wherever there are palms. It relies on the skill of a palm 'tapper' to release the juice from the palm's trunk and collect it before carefully preparing it to ferment using yeasts in the air, for as little as a couple of hours in some cases. Within a day it's ready to drink as a fresh alcoholic beverage ranging from 4 per cent ABV upwards (and significantly more when distilled). Control of palm wine, given the lengthy process it took to tap and collect it, and its short shelf life, was a show of power and influence. It was mostly younger men who tapped the wine, and tappers were expected to send a pot of wine to their leader each day. A Twi proverb (Twi is the language of the Akan kingdoms) succinctly articulates the link between wealth and access to alcohol in Ashanti culture, which used cowrie shells from the Indian ocean as currency: 'When you do not have cowrie shells, then you say wine is not sweet.'[i]

---

i Emmanuel Kwaku Akyeampong, *Drink, Power, and Cultural Change: A Social History of Alcohol in Ghana, c. 1800 to Recent Times* (Oxford: Currey, 1996), p. 40.

From the eighteenth century onwards the Ashanti opened trading relations with Europeans, who increasingly came to the west coast with the principal aim of the forceful trading of low-value manufactured (and sometimes broken or outdated) goods in a barbaric exchange for enslaved Africans, as well as gold and ivory and raw materials like gum (from rubber plants) and timber. Increasing incursions into neighbouring territories by merchants and then states from Europe established permanent footings on the coast, and in 1821 Britain annexed the neighbouring coastal territory of the Ashanti in what would become the Gold Coast Colony.

Eventually these incursions came for the Ashanti too and they fought the British in a series of five wars from 1823 onwards. In 1874 the capital Kumasi was captured and burned to the ground by British troops but uprisings by the Ashanti continued until 1902, when Ashanti leaders and British forces negotiated the annexation of the kingdom as a protectorate of the Gold Coast Colony on the condition that the Golden Stool, its royal house, would remain. Shortly afterwards the same Ashanti royals were exiled to the Seychelles and Ashanti loyalists hid the Golden Stool for safekeeping; it would only re-emerge in 1920.

From the mid 1940s onwards an emerging middle class was striving for independence; returning veterans from the war added to this clamour. From 1946 a semblance of political representation was introduced with half of the council being elected, although the council remained secondary to the governor. Farmers, the middle classes and veterans began a campaign of disruptive action which evolved into a political movement calling for independence. From this emergent independence movement emerged Ghana's first formal political independence vehicles, first through the United Gold Coast Convention movement in 1947 and then the Convention People's Party (CCP) in 1949. The latter party which would lead Ghana to independence a decade and a half later was pioneered by the charismatic, anti-colonial leader Kwame Nkrumah.

A graduate of two US universities and veteran of the Pan-African Congress Movement, Nkrumah sought to push for independence not through intellectual political groups but by chiming with the needs and desires of ordinary people, winning support among veterans, youths, farmers and the most influential of social movers, powerful female market traders. Following a brief imprisonment, he entered government, though subordinate to the British Governor-General, on the back of his party winning a huge majority in the first ever legislative elections in the Gold Coast in 1951.

Nkrumah and the CCP continued their popular push for full independence and democracy, sometimes in the face of resistance from older local elite structures, until 1957 when Ghana gained self-rule as a dominion and then became a republic in 1960.

Taste(s) of the gods, palm wine, akpeteshie and imported spirits

In Ghana's Akan mythology from the Fante people, palm wine was discovered by one of the king's hunters, called Ansa, who encountered a fallen palm that had been bored down by an elephant which had used its tusks to break open the trunk and drink from the sap. Wisely, Ansa tested the sap first on his dog, who evidently liked it enough that Ansa then tried it. In fact, Ansa went well beyond trying it, he quickly became drunk. After trying the drink he learned how to tap palms and gathered enough to take to the king. The king drank the whole pot in one go and happily nodded off. Rather unhappily for Ansa, however, the king's sleep was so deep and undisturbed that the royal courtiers presumed him dead and Ansa a murderer. Ansa was quickly dispatched for poisoning the king, before the king could wake up and prevent the lasting damage of the confusion. Yet Ansa did leave behind his name for the drink: '*nsa*' in Twi.

In most palm wine origin myths in the region, the narrative of sleeping like the dead and awakening is always present, as is the death of the discoverer or drinker of the wine, illustrating the concept of palm wine as a spiritual medium linking the living and the dead.

As trade with Europeans increased from the eighteenth century onwards so too did the influence of far stronger European spirits, which were treated as a form of currency and drunk and amalgamated into traditional worship practices. One Ashanti noble recalled how the colours of brands of European spirits had appealed to the traditions associated with different local deities. For example, the Ashanti war god preferred the colour of Buccaneer rum as it evoked spiritual myths of gods drinking the blood of their nemeses, while other gods were more discerning, with the god of rainfall and good harvest preferring the purity of gin and schnapps.

Drinking rituals and palm wine culture

Ashanti sources show a range of interesting and eyebrow-raising rituals and customs which used alcohol, traditionally palm wine but also imported spirits, liberally. Generally the use of alcohol was reserved for elders and elites, outside of its use in traditional customs, which mostly marked the significant moments in life like birth, coming of age, marriage and death.

When a baby was born in the Ashanti kingdoms it was traditional to give it an initial name and then eight days later a formal naming ceremony would take place. It was understood that this gap was to allow the child to leave its spirit-world mother behind and make its way to the world of the living and its birth mother. The journey from the spirit world was arduous, so much so that newborns were given a tiny drop of rum with lime (it was likely to have been palm wine pre-European trade) to refresh them. Eight days later the child had fully left the spirit world and was given a full name; at that point the child was handed to the father, who gave the baby another refreshing drop of rum and if the name given was the same as that of an ancestor then wine was brought and offered to the spirit of the ancestor to bless the use of the name.

Palm wine and gin were also central in a women-only ceremony which celebrated the coming of age of a woman in pre-Christian Ashanti society. When young women had their first period, their mother would hold a libation party and invite all the women in the area, who collectively asked for a blessing that the now woman would safely have children, offering the sky god a libation of palm wine. Then all the women of the settlement would meet, drink palm wine, gin or rum and ban men from the public space for the day. It is suggested that these gatherings were a place where women would drink uproariously, with palm wine usually reserved for male elders; scold and make fun of their respective husbands' flaws; and play drums and dance through the night to daybreak.[ii]

Just as the start and major shifts in life were marked with ritual drinking, so too was the end of life. In Ashanti society, funerals were a serious and seriously boozy business, involving several days of mourning with libations and fasting – a dangerous combination.

After a beloved's passing, a lament was given in their dwelling before the body was laid for all to view and palm wine brought before the burial. For the funeral itself guests would fast from food but drink palm wine; it was in this period that the deceased was believed to be between the spirit and physical worlds. The intoxication of guests was considered a way to bridge the worlds and ease the passing of the departed/ing.

From burial, for a further seven days mourners would drink and make offerings of alcohol. This would then be repeated on the fifteenth and fortieth day after the funeral. For the Ashanti, however, death was far from final and the dead were always close, between their departure to the spirit world and their eventual reincarnation. The culture of the stool, in which the wooden seats of ancestors were kept, meant the departed were never too far away, and in the Ashanti New Year rum was sprinkled on all the quarters of the dead elders, a festivity known as *homowo*.

---

ii Emmanuel Kwaku Akyeampong, *Drink, Power, and Cultural Change*, p. 36.

Liberation games with akpeteshie

In the early twentieth century Gold Coast alcohol duties were put up and imports restricted, both deliberately to raise funds and in response to shortages caused by the First World War. As a consequence, the backyard production of illicit akpeteshie, which in Ga (one of Ghana's local languages) means 'they are hiding', became an unstoppable craze which would take hold of the country. As the name suggests, this distilled palm-wine spirit was increasingly made across the colony in secret, filling the gap left by more expensive and hard-to-find European spirits for traditional, recreational and revolutionary uses.

To make akpeteshie one requires only a simple kit of bottles, large containers such as oil drums or a dugout boat, a fire and some piping and, crucially, a lot of palm wine. To make 25 litres of palm spirit a minimum of 300 litres of palm wine is required, which is boiled down and vaporised twice to create the desired strength. Despite the legal risks, the technique caught on in a big way, and distilled palm spirit was quickly popular across West Africa. In the British Colony of the Gold Coast, akpeteshie came to be the tipple that tipped the balance, fuelling (sometimes literally) the change which brought independence from Britain and upset more traditional social orders.

It helped distil a change in social dynamics in cities and towns across the Gold Coast, known as the highlife in the 1930s, when a new class of workers and middle-class clerical people was emerging. Fuelled by akpeteshie, this activity included the fusion music of European jazz and Ashanti traditional melodies (many such songs were written about akpeteshie and how to get around its official ban) and new forms of entertainment, including a type of comic opera called 'concert' for which full evening dress would be required. This emergent group of young urban people, as well as First World War veterans, were cut off from rural expectations and social structures and created a buzz which uprooted society in the colony.

> Highlife music is a blend of early- to mid-twentieth-century jazz, foxtrot and traditional West African melodies. Emerging among brass bands in the late nineteenth century, Gold Coast highlife came to take on more musical instruments of European origin and African percussion. By the 1950s it had spread into neighbouring Nigeria and took on Trinidadian calypso rhythms to fuse a pan-Atlantic musical sound which remains a hugely popular legacy in Ghana today and influenced musical trends that followed, including contemporary Afrobeat. Ghanaian workers brought the highlife sound to Sierra Leone and Liberia, where today it is literally called 'palm wine music' and is played in coastal bars where rhythms and influences from all shores mingle.

When it came to enjoying akpeteshie, though, the British had other ideas and continued to ban and destroy any production of the distilled palm-wine spirit they could find in the colony. The issue of being unable to make or drink akpeteshie would quickly become symbolic of the wider issue faced by ordinary people: that of unjustifiable and overbearing British rule. When the colonial government tried to raise a tax to make up for the loss of alcohol duties in 1929, local chiefs wrote back advising against it given the popular anger it would cause.

The laws were passed anyway and the anticipated anger spilled onto the streets, and onto the shelves as the already restricted alcohol imports fell even further this time due to boycotts, as did government revenues. The government tried in vain to introduce beer as a less strong and more centrally controllable beverage but akpeteshie was so popular and so easy to make that it didn't catch on. Thousands of illicit distillers smuggled akpeteshie into towns to fuel the bustling social scene and shipping embargoes during the Second World War stifled alternative imports even further. Akpeteshie was by then the unassailable spirit of the emerging independence movement and also the bellwether everyday issue which united soon-to-be Ghanaians behind it.

Following the war, the clamour for independence grew and grew, interlinked with the issue of akpeteshie, which exemplified the hated British rule. These vexations got ordinary people out onto the streets to call first for the right to distil akpeteshie and later for independence. In 1948 in Accra, young men organised a revivalist festival and under the guise of drunkenness marched and confronted police to protest British rule. The police put the revolt down brutally, killing several protestors.

By the time the second elections were held in 1954, Nkrumah, as head of the people's party CCP, was wildly popular and his campaign was driven by and focused on akpeteshie. Hit songs by top Gold Coast artists clamoured for Nkrumah to bring about self-rule – The Comets' 'Nkrumah Special' – and for the legalisation of akpeteshie – Okaja Coal Boys' 'Don't Say That It Isn't Good' or The

Comets' 'Akpeteshie'. CCP campaigns themselves drew in crowds for fundraising dances with the promise that 'an inexhaustible bar will be run' and opened up bars for Ghanaian women too.[iii]

Independence came in 1957, but it wasn't until 1962, when akpeteshie distilling was legalised, that Ghanaians could finally legally drink the spirit of independence. Today akpeteshie is enjoyed liberally in Ghana and used recreationally and in traditional toasts. What it now lacks in political fire, it still makes up for in its fiery strength.

How to drink akpeteshie and palm wine; Ghanaian highlife style

To get the very best from your glass of palm wine or akpeteshie, I wholeheartedly suggest throwing a palm wine and akpeteshie highlife bash, involving the best of the trends of Gold Coast's roaring thirties, at least for its urban middle classes.

Number of players: As many as you like, and none that you don't.

You will need:
- Glad rags, bright dresses, suits and top hats.
- A playlist of the best of Ghana's highlife music, including top hits from:
  o Kwame Asare

[iii] Emmanuel Kwaku Akyeampong, *Drink, Power, and Cultural Change*, p. 128.

- o The Comets
- o E. T. Mensah
- o Cape Coast Sugar Babies
- o Accra Orchestra
- o Kofi Ghanaba
- Large quantities of palm wine and akpeteshie.
- Comic opera scripts and some willing/budding/begrudging friends to play them.
- A selection of popular Ghanaian dishes, barbecue:
  - o Jollof (we have no comment on the origin debate here, we just like it)
  - o Plantain
  - o Tilapia
  - o Yam or Cassava

How to play:
1. Gather your friends, who by this point in you reading this text must be thoroughly exhausted with all you've put them through. Nonetheless they will no doubt persevere, so once you've gathered them and they've gathered themselves, set out a bit of the background to Ghanaian highlife music.
2. School over, you can break open the akpeteshie and get on with the comic opera, accompanied perhaps with Ghanaian jollof, fufu, plantain and fish. And if at the end of it you aren't quite feeling the opera it's perhaps easier if you just have a nice barbecue.

Jiuling and Fifty-Two Gifts

China's Amazing Array of Drinking Games and the Invention of Playing Cards, 4000 BCE–1911 CE

Chinese influence in the pastime of Touhu in ancient Korea was but one enduring legacy of a rich history of drinking games which have formed a central part of Chinese culture for thousands of years. Confucian arrow-flinging aside, Chinese drinking games range from high literary battles of wit and poetry to the backstreet battles of finger wars. These games evolved from both the courts of great emperors and the rooms and streets of ordinary people.

From the very earliest known alcoholic drinks in Chinese winemaking to the hard spirits and most popular beers on the planet today, a range of Chinese drinking games, known collectively as Jiuling, have been an integral part of Chinese drinking customs. Jiuling can broadly be separated into two groups of drinking games: the high culture or 'elegant games' and lower culture 'popular games'. Elegant games included literary, poetic, dramatic, and riddle-based challenges with strong rule-based codes and heavy drinking forfeits; popular drinking games, played by those well versed in the school of life rather than noble or scholarly disciplines, often were more robust, used more skill, chance and speed and were (probably) much more fun, all told.

In this chapter we will look past the Confucian game of Touhu, which originated in China, and into the plethora of games that stayed in and were played in ancient China. We'll also examine perhaps China's greatest gift to the world of games, drinking and otherwise: the invention of playing cards as a consequence of Jiuling. Yes, dear reader, from the tense halls across the world playing bridge, euchre or canasta to the glitz of Macau, Las Vegas or Monaco, and the regional variants of decks in Italy, Germany, Spain and Portugal, every game of cards you've played or been bemused by, wondering at the obscure and poorly remembered rules, all of them derive from Jiuling, Chinese drinking games.

The most ancient and the most consumed

Wine in China has an ancient history, as old perhaps as the hills, with legends variously accounting its origin to monkeys fermenting fruit in caves, or to one man called Tu K'ang who historian Mu-Chou notes rather unhelpfully we know literally nothing about, or to a mistake in the time of the Ancient Kings when someone accidentally left some rice to ferment in an empty trunk.[i]

Wine is usually the term referred to in translations of Chinese texts, but to the modern sommelier this might be seen as an affront to the grape most commonly used in global wine production today. Wine is often used to refer to all types of alcoholic drinks in ancient China, often made from millet or rice or sometimes fermented fruits. In fact, Western grape wine was not introduced to China until the Han dynasty in around 200 BCE; however, wild eastern grape varieties existed in China and were used for winemaking, alongside other ingredients, from 7000 BCE.

A Neolithic village called Jiahu in China's Henan province holds a very important record, that of the earliest known alcoholic beverage, 9,000 years ago. Jars excavated from this ancient site held chemical traces of the tipples they contained, which were found to be a mix of rice wine, fermented honey, hawthorn and wild grape fruits.[ii]

From these early beginnings, Chinese drinking culture grew and delivered the most popular of beverages some 2,000 years later, a normally rice-based drink which used wild yeasts to ferment into alcohol. This was known as *jiu* and was most popular in its sweetened form *huangjiu*, which translates as 'yellow wine'. Beloved of poets and painters, though sometimes frowned upon by philosophical schools, it was ubiquitous across all levels of Chinese society through China's 'golden age'.

---

i Mu-Chou Poo, 'The Use and Abuse of Wine in Ancient China'. *Journal of the Economic and Social History of the Orient*, 42, no. 2 (1999): p. 123.
ii Nadia Durrani, 'Oldest Wine from Jiahu, China', *World Archaeology*.

To make *huangjiu* the rice must first be soaked in water, traditionally for up to twenty days, and then steamed. After steaming the rice is mixed with the two most crucial ingredients of *huangjiu*: wild yeast and a starter culture derived from wheat known as *qu*. *Qu* particularly helps create the unique microbiome conditions which give *huangjiu* its celebrated flavour profile. This mixture is brewed under controlled temperatures for two months and even the smallest change in the process results in a different-flavoured drink, while significant variation can totally spoil the production. This sensitivity to different temperatures meant regional variations in *huangjiu* were common during its artisanal production, though modern techniques today are reducing that diversity.[iii]

At around the same time as Western cultures were experimenting with distillation to strengthen grape wine, China, then under the rule of the Ming dynasty, also developed stills and, taking *haungjiu*, through distillation created *shaojiu*, translated as 'burnt wine' – or, as it is known today, *baijiu*, translated as 'white spirit' (not turpentine!). This fermented grain spirit diversified and was taken up and changed in localities across China, while the sweet grain wine also retained popularity, especially for the wealthy. As China, becoming the People's Republic of China in 1949, industrialised, the production of *baijiu* moved from artisanal distillation to controlled production and was increasingly mass produced as a spirit of the people.[iv]

Today *baijiu* is the world's best-selling and most consumed spirit, with an apparent 10.8 billion litres

---

iii Mu-Chou Poo, 'The Use and Abuse of Wine in Ancient China'
iv Unknown author, *The Story of Baijiu*, Drink Baijiu.

consumed in China.^v That's equivalent to the volume of New Zealand's largest lake, Lake Taupo, which is 238 square miles by surface area.

Drinks, games and the creation of cards

The 9,000+ years of drinking in China has unsurprisingly given birth to a great range of drinking games and pastimes. Touhu or pitch pot, as we read earlier, emerged in China before gaining popularity in medieval Korea, but control of alcohol consumption in any form, game or otherwise, was a clear concern of its rulers across millennia. When the Zhou dynasty came to power it was said that alcoholism had been the downfall of the Shang dynasty and it was briefly touted that the abuse of indulgence in wine would be punishable by death.[vi]

This thankfully didn't catch on, as it is clearly evidenced that from the Zhou period (1200–731 BCE) drinking games, Jiuling, were routinely played at banquets, and a drink, usually of wine, remained the 'punishment'; it's notable that this 'punishment' probably made the Jiuling very popular. In fact, it was this concern about drinking culture which brought forward Jiuling during the Zhou period as a way to regulate drinking etiquette to avoid excess, mainly by focusing on how and when and in what manner a toast could be made. Over time these toasts grew as methods of

---

v Pauline Froissart and Dan Martin, 'Tough Sell: Baijiu, China's. Potent Tipple, Looks Abroad', *The Jakarta Post*, 18 June 2019.
vi Mu-Chou Poo, 'The Use and Abuse of Wine in Ancient China', p. 129.

demonstrating wit and intellectual prowess and, also, a way to merrily drink to increasing excess. They formed complex rules and methods, and met and mirrored more popular drinking games played in taverns and festivals: these together formed the two branches of Jiuling.

The birth of card games

Before we dive headlong into the dizzy depths of ancient Jiuling, we must take a brief detour into perhaps its greatest offspring: the birth (though debated) of modern playing cards. Some forms of Jiuling in ancient China, also known as the 'ale rules' or the 'game of leaves', evolved to have a set of written instructions to guide or instruct a turn taker in their individual game task. Each instruction was often written on an individual tab or flat-edged stick, though the surviving (fancy) examples include a silver vase on the back of a silver turtle with individual silver instruction 'tabs'. These instructions were sometimes literary rules for the rich, but among ordinary Chinese a version with much simpler and more directly inebriating rules developed, known simply as 'wine cards', which gave simple instructions to a player of how many cups they or another player should drink.

Wine cards are still used today in modern-day Sichuan, and along with the emergence of tile-based games like dominoes and mah-jong in ancient China, these games are thought to have given rise to the development of playing cards during the ninth century CE under the Tang dynasty. At this time they quickly spread and evolved both in western Asia and Europe as well as in China, developing suits, colours and ever more parameters which enabled more complex and engaging gameplay.

The first recorded cards in Europe are a set given to the King of France by the Spanish ambassador in 1377, but to get to Europe, early cards passed first through the Middle East along trade routes known collectively as the Silk Road from ancient China to the West. They spread to the Mameluke Empire in Egypt, which created suits of goblets, coins, swords and polo mallets; on their journey across the Mediterranean European traders dropped the weird long mallets, not knowing then what polo was, and replaced them with wooden stakes or clubs. These then formed the traditional suits which are still found today in Spain, and in some of the seventeen styles of playing cards which Italy preserves to this day. As cards moved north, further varieties developed, such as German, Dutch and English cards, with the development of the fifty-two-card deck used today in the Anglophone world. The oldest surviving fifty-two-card deck (from 1475 in the Netherlands) can be seen today in New York's Metropolitan Museum of Art, while the earliest records of cards in China date from some 200 years before that.

Cards and the invention of them can then be rooted in the drinking games, Jiuling, of ancient China, but were then rapidly melded and moulded to and by cultures that picked them up and played with them across the deserts, seas and plains of the great Silk Road routes, eventually settling into a myriad of different localised versions across the great Eurasian landmass in a little over two centuries.

Elegant games or literary Jiuling

Jiuling first emerged among elite groups in ancient Chinese society who corrupted and re-engineered social rules on toasting etiquette to create a complex web of intellectual and pompous games of riddles, rhyme and wit, which would pit players against each other as well as their own tolerance for rice wine. These games were known as elegant or literary Jiuling; numerous versions of these complex games are recorded but we will focus on a handful here.

Fishing for the giant sea turtle

This curiously titled game required a vessel or jar within which were metal tabs containing inscriptions or poems, each of these known as a fish. Before gameplay a poem was read:

> The immortal giant sea turtles at the bottom of the sea are difficult to match,
> They carry a golden peak which is Yangzhou Paradise
> How did the giant from Elder Dragon Kingdom fish for turtles then?
> He used a rainbow for a long rod, and the crescent moon for a hook.[vii]

Players would sit some distance from the bowl and take it in turns to try to catch two 'fish' with a rod. Once the fish

---

[vii] Andrew Lo, 'The Game of Leaves: An Inquiry into the Origin of Chinese Playing Cards', *Bulletin of the School of Oriental and African Studies* 63, no. 3 (2000): p. 397.

were caught the player had to read out and perform the instruction or poem. One example instruction informed the reader to: 'Please use the fine examinations to drink a full ten units.'[viii] This game was popular in the Song period, and the recorder of it notes that in his time (1175–1231 CE) people left the fishing part of the game behind and just drew diagrams of drinking penalties and passed poems and instructions to one another. This game and other similar games derived from it (the game of gathering pearls was a similar game which used tokens, 'Pearls', with instructions to inform drinking and other player actions and forfeits) were expressly designed to urge people to drink. A beautiful set of a later version of the game, sadly no longer including the rods like rainbows with crescent moons for hooks, does survive today. Wrought out of silver metal, the set is fashioned as a jar atop the shell of a large metal turtle and fifty inscribed metal sticks or 'tallies' (replacing fish) are included within the jar from which players pick.

Anyatang Jiuling: drinking orders from the hall of peace and elegance

This game, recorded by one Cao Shao, involved a hundred or more drinking instructions and poems, with an even larger selection of 120 or so in a later Ming-period version.[ix] The instructions were essentially stage directions. The example below is an instruction card which followed the reciting of a poem about pulling at a woman's robe at a party:

viii Lo, 'The Game of Leaves', p. 397.
ix Lo, 'The Game of Leaves', p. 400.

Card #55:
Extinguish the candles at the banquet. In a while, no matter
if there are courtesans around or not, everyone is allowed to say a rude
phrase, but they cannot take advantage of the moment to move their hands.
If it is the daytime and there are no candles, everyone closes his or her
eyes and still has to say a dirty phrase. The person who gets this command
drinks a cup secretly to apologise for pulling at the clothes of the beauty.[x]

The game of the green bower novel

Other versions of elegant or literary Jiuling included riddles or tongue-twisters, many of which are given as examples in ancient Chinese literature, including one novel known as *The Dream of the Green Bower*. In this game characters again draw a wooden piece from a group of a hundred or so with a drink-related instruction. The first player to draw a piece begins a popular game known as *shuangsheng* (translated as 'twin sounds') in which each piece drawn has on it words related to physical things such as animals, stars, myths or plants, and in addition to the phrase the player can choose alliteration or rhyme. Choice made, the speaker must then recite a classical, philosophical or historical quotation related to the subject of their inscription in alliteration or rhyme. Once this small feat

---

[x] Lo, 'The Game of Leaves', p. 400.

has been accomplished the player then chooses a significant word in their recited quote to instruct another player to drink, using the beginning or end character of the word (here the specific mechanisms and structures of Mandarin make translating the game difficult). Essentially, the player picked must make a form of rhyme or alliteration related to the commanding phrase, take a drink and then a turn.[xi] Got that?

Popular Jiuling or 'common' (fun) games

If your head is spinning from the witty, worldly and wacky games of ancient China's most exclusive literary drinking circles, then fear not, as from here on we examine the Jiuling of the people, the drinking games of the street, sometimes referred to, disparagingly in our view, as common Jiuling. As we read above, the earliest cards, 'wine cards' (sometimes known as *Eight Immortals wine cards* which survive today as the traditional *Zi Pai* Chinese deck), can be considered among these games but they remain just one example of a great procession of popular Jiuling left to us from ancient and medieval China.

---

xi Li Guo, 'The Courtesans' Drinking Games in "The Dream in the Green Bower"', in *Games and Play in Chinese and Sinophone Cultures*, Li Guo, Douglas Eyman and Hongmei Sun (eds) (Seattle: University of Washington Press, 2024), pp. 117–20.

Popular ale rules

A less literary version of the ale rules, *lyling*, used chip counters made of bamboo to tally the drinks consumed per player in each round. According to one source Jiuling of the popular variety still had a structure and set of rules similar to other forms of Jiuling but with a clearer focus: to ensure that guests at drinking bouts did as they were instructed. The source, Huang Pusong's Tang dynasty monograph *The Drunken Days and Nights,* lists how a drinking observer armed with dice and a wine scoop, a drinking keeper and an over-drinking executor (who dolled out the punishment of more wine for over-drinking) could be employed to enable drinking games. Each chip counter would include tasks that the player who picked it must act out. The rest of the group would then decide if the performance of the instruction was sufficient; if not, then the performer had to finish their glass of wine.[xii]

Toupan

Toupan, translated as 'to toss a die', was a very simple game – if a game at all – which determined the order of drinking. Each player roles a die and keeps their number; thereafter when that number is rolled the player with the matching number drinks.

---

xii Yao Wan and Thawascha Dechsubha, 'A Survey of Traditional Chinese Drinking Games', *Technium Social Sciences Journal*, vol. 31, no. 1 (2022): pp. 728–41.

Gong show

In this popular ancient game a flower is passed around a group to the beat of a gong. As the game progresses the beat increases and intensifies until it is stopped suddenly and without warning. The player left holding the flower when the gong stops has to drink, and then the game continues. There is no recorded end to the game but one can imagine when gameplay is no longer viable.

Paoda or Finger guessing

In this game, opposing players would strike out their hands with a certain number of fingers extended. At the same time the player opposite would guess the number of fingers their opposing player held out; if they guessed correctly the 'finger thrower' would drink, whereas they would drink if they guessed incorrectly. This deceptively simple game remains hugely popular and evolves quickly, with an experienced player, into a complex game of bluffing, code and counter-bluffing to outmanoeuvre the opposition.

Modern Jiuling

Today in China, drinking games remain a central part of social and drinking culture, often in business circles. The extensive heritage of Jiuling from ancient China has filtered down and some games, though sadly not 'Fishing for the Giant Sea Turtle with Rainbow Rods Hooked with Crescent Moons', are still played today, including gong show, Paoda (finger guessing) and later versions of dice games, too. A hugely popular modern Jiuling is that of Chui Niu, a form of liar's dice where players must roll dice in secret and then make a claim as to their value; at the next round of claims and throws the value should increase and if one player thinks another is lying to get a higher dice value number they can shout 'bu xing', but if they're wrong then they must finish their glass.

China, then, perhaps holds the undisputed crown of drinking games, from their earliest roots in the ancient tavern in the village of Jihau 9,000 years ago, through the invention and proliferation of rice wines and later rice spirits, to the development of complex and perhaps onerous literary games in court circles for thousands of years. The shattering of the old Chinese order in the twentieth century – from the 1911 Xinhai Revolution to the Chinese Civil War and the establishment of the People's Republic in 1949 after the victory of the Chinese Communist Party – shifted the focus of drinking games from the elite to the masses as they industrialised the production of alcohol in China. It's a complex history that threads through China's dynasties and emperors with the offshoots of Jiuling leaving impressions in China and the rest of the world today through the related development of playing cards, of dominoes and mah-jong too. With so many to choose from it leaves the contemporary researcher/practitioner an almost dangerous dilemma of which, and how many, to attempt and at what cost.

How to Jiuling

Number of players: Is there really anyone you know now who is still willing and eager to try one of these? If so, choose any of the remaining acquaintances you can muster.

You will need:

For all games:
- Chinese rice wine *huangjiu*.
- Chinese rice spirit *baijiu*.
- Chinese beer (as an alternative option to the above, though Chinese beer is a relatively modern addition to China's indigenous beverages).

For gong show:
- A gong, something showy that makes a big impact, think wrought metal, dragons, etc.
- A flower; for something in keeping with the origin of the game you could choose chrysanthemum, camellia, magnolia or plum blossom.

For common and literary versions of the ale rules:
- A great bowl in which to place inscribed sticks.
- Wide lollipop sticks, or something more upmarket if you prefer.
- Fine pen to inscribe the sticks with specific poems, phrases, literary mischief and, crucially, drinking instructions.
- To adapt for Fishing for the Giant Sea Turtle, add rainbow rods with crescent moons.

For other miscellaneous poetic Jiuling (if you dare):
- A compendium of Chinese literary, philosophical,

historical or other cultural quotations and knowledge. For a comparative companion in English literary culture, try something like *Brewer's Dictionary of Phrase and Fable*.

How to play (and first pick what to play):
Faced with such a range of games from ancient China and the limited patience of any of your remaining friends to engage in yet another 'fun' ancient drinking game, I would recommend that the considered reader tries but two of the many Jiuling of ancient China.

The instructions for the games are broadly outlined within the chapter above but the question of literary or popular games is one major dilemma faced by the host of any Jiuling party. Given the choice, I'd wager that thousands of years of Chinese drinking culture is unlikely to be wrong in calling one of these 'popular'; they're probably a good deal more fun!

> **Top tip:** a modern twist on the ales rules can mix literary Jiuling with more popular Jiuling, with cards instructing players to 'finger battle', quickly play 'gong show' or undertake silly tasks for the judgement of the group. In addition players pick an ancient pearl of wisdom related to the subject of the card and then develop an alliterative rhyme which others must follow with a related recital or face the penalty of drinking wine.

Bibliography

The sources used to inform this book are almost all secondary and I built upon the hard work and dedication of brilliant historians and scholars who collected, interpreted and presented the findings of their (sometimes quirky) enquiries in so many interesting ways. Any error in the presentation of their work is entirely my own and I and all of us owe them a debt as creators of knowledge, as we do the librarians and curators who keep it.

Chapter 1

Ancient Greece, *Encyclopaedia Britannica*, https://www.britannica.com/place/ancient-Greece [accessed 9 July 2024]

Athenaeus: Deipnosophistae, Book 15, *Attalus*, http://www.attalus.org/old/athenaeus15a.html [accessed 25 June 2024]

Cartwright, Mark, 'Wine in the Ancient Mediterranean', *World History Encyclopedia*, 2 September 2009, https://www.worldhistory.org/article/944/wine-in-the-ancient-mediterranean/ [accessed 6 July 2024]

Csapo, E. and Miller, M. C., 'The "Kottabos-Toast" and an Inscribed Red-Figured Cup', *Hesperia*, 60.3 (1991), pp. 367–82, https://doi.org/10.2307/148071 [accessed 12 February 2023]

'Drinking Cup (Kylix)', *The J. Paul Getty Museum*, https://www.getty.edu/art/collection/object/103VNT?altImage=027feae8-ae61-4775-a322-f98830cbf5f4 [accessed 14 July 2024]

'Kylix Depicting an Erotic Scene', *David Aaron Gallery*, https://davidaaron.com/artworks/kylix-depicting-an-erotic-scene/ [accessed 18 June 2024]

Lissarrague, François, *The Aesthetics of the Greek Banquet: Drinking Games*, trans. Andrew Szegedy-Maszak (Princeton: Princeton University Press, 1990), pp. 80–86

Pindar, *Fragments*, Loeb Classical Library, https://www.loebclassics.com/view/pindar-fragments/1997/pb_LCL485.373.xml? [accessed 5 July 2024]

Pruitt, Sarah, 'Ancient Greek Drinking Game Makes a Comeback', *Live Science*, 2 March 2015, https://www.livescience.com/49441-greek-drinking-game-kottabos-recreated.html [accessed 20 June 2024]

Rosen, Ralph M., 'Euboulos' *Ankylion* and the Game of Kottabos', *The Classical Quarterly*, 39.2 (1989), pp. 355–9, http://www.jstor.org/stable/639378 [accessed 12 February 2023]

Scaife, Ross, 'From Kottabos to War in Aristophanes' *Acharnians*', *Greek, Roman and Byzantine Studies*, 33.1 (1992), pp. 25–33

Vickers, Michael, 'A Kottabos Cup in Oxford', *American Journal of Archaeology*, 78.2 (1974), p. 158, https://www.journals.uchicago.edu/doi/abs/10.2307/502803 [accessed 14 July 2024]

Chapter 2

Achilleos, Stella, 'Drinking and Good Fellowship: Alehouse Communities and the Anxiety of Social Dislocation in Broadside Ballads of the 1620s and 1630s', *Early Modern Literary Studies*, 20.1 (2014), pp. 1–32, https://www.academia.edu/108802908/Drinking_and_Good_Fellowship_Alehouse_Communities_and_the_Anxiety_of_Social_Dislocation_in_Broadside_Ballads_of_the_1620s_and_1630s [accessed 9 June 2024]

Achilleos, Stella, 'Puzzle Jugs in the Regency', *The Regency Redingote*, 3 July 2009, https://regencyredingote.wordpress.com/2009/07/03/puzzle-jugs-in-the-regency/ [accessed 28 May 2024]

The Brewery History Society, 'Alcohol in the Early Modern World: A Cultural History', *Brewery History*, 150 (2013), pp. 39–53

'Fuddling Cup', The Metropolitan Museum of Art, https://www.metmuseum.org/art/collection/search/196568 [accessed 26 May 2024]

Fumerton, Patricia and Guerrini, Anita (eds) with Kris McAbee, *Ballads and Broadsides in Britain, 1500–1800* (London: Ashgate, 2010)

'Puzzle Jug', *British Archaeology*, Ashmolean Museum, https://britisharchaeology.ashmus.ox.ac.uk/highlights/puzzle-jug.html [accessed 7 June 2024]

'Puzzle Jug', Victoria and Albert Museum, https://collections.vam.ac.uk/item/O21042/fuddling-cup-unknown/ [accessed 30 May 2024]

Mark Hailwood, '"Come Hear This Ditty": Seventeenth-Century Drinking Songs and Hearing the Past', *The Appendix*, vol. 1, no. 3 (2013), https://theappendix.net/issues/2013/7/come-hear-this-ditty-seventeenth-century-drinking-songs-and-hearing-the-past [accessed 17 April 2024]

Hailwood, Mark, '"It Puts Good Reason into Brains": Popular Understandings of the Effects of Alcohol in Seventeenth-Century England', *Brewery History*, 150 (2013), pp. 39–53

Standley, Eleanor R., '"Ffylle the Cuppe and Make vs Mery": Lobed Drinking Vessels and their Use in Later Medieval England', *Medieval Archaeology*, 68.1 (2024), pp. 102–138, https://doi.org/10.1080/00766097.2024.2350194 [accessed 8 May 2024]

Withington, Phil, 'Intoxicants and Society in Early Modern England', *The Historical Journal*, 54.3 (2011), pp. 631–57, http://www.jstor.org/stable/23017266 [accessed 9 June 2024]

The English Broadside Ballad Archive, *EBBA*, https://ebba.english.ucsb.edu/ballad/30416/xml [accessed 21 May 2024]

Tlusty, B. Ann (ed.), *Alcohol in the Early Modern World: A Cultural History* (London: Bloomsbury Academic, 2021), https://www.bloomsbury.com/uk/alcohol-in-the-early-modern-world-9781350199620/ [accessed 9 June 2024]

Chapter 3

Bailey, Natasha Kate, *Nahua Communities in the Pulque Trade of Early Colonial Mexico, 1550–1668* (PhD thesis, University of Leicester, 2021)

Bumbar, Micky, 'Pulque and the Devil: A Mexican Folk Tale', *Lords of the Drinks*, https://lordsofthedrinks.org/2018/06/16/the-pulque-vendor-and-the-devil-a-mexican-folk-tale/ [accessed 26 May 2024]

Córdova, James M., 'Drinking the Fifth Cup: Notes on the Drunken Indian Image in Colonial Mexico', *Word & Image*, 31.1 (2015), pp. 1–18

DiCesare, Dr Catherine R., 'The Aztec Approach to Alcohol', *Mexicolore*, https://www.mexicolore.co.uk/aztecs/home/the-aztec-approach-to-alcohol [accessed 16 June 2024]

Henderson, Lucia, 'Blood, Water, Vomit, and Wine', *Mesoamerican Voices*, 3 (2008), pp. 53–68, http://journals.uic.edu/mv [accessed 10 June 2024]

Hellmuth, Nicholas and Toralla, María José, 'Enema Rituals of the Classic Maya and Nearby Cultures of Mesoamerica: Bibliography and Suggested Reading', *FLAAR Mesoamerica*, September 2022, https://flaar-mesoamerica.org/wp-content/uploads/2022/09/enema-bibliography-for-PDF-in-September-Hellmuth-and-Toralla-2022-Sep-15-2022-NH-MJT.pdf [accessed 25 June 2024]

Maestri, Nicoletta, 'Pulque, Ancient Mesoamerican Sacred Drink', *ThoughtCo.*, 12 November 2019, https://www.thoughtco.com/the-origin-of-pulque-170882 [accessed 21 June 2024]

Tomky, Naomi, 'The Drink of the Gods: An Introduction to Pulque', *Serious Eats*, 25 May 2023, https://www.seriouseats.com/introduction-to-pulque [accessed 17 June 2024]

Toner, Deborah, 'Pulque: Ritual and Power in Aztec Mexico', *Consuming Authenticities*, https://staffblogs.le.ac.uk/consumingauthenticities/2015/07/03/the-story-of-pulque-part-3-ritual-and-power-in-aztec-mexico/ [accessed 7 May 2024]

Wyatt, Andrew R., *The Food and Cuisine of Precolumbian Mesoamerica* (Mexico City: Wyatt Publishing, 2021)

Mesoamerican Civilization, *Encyclopaedia Britannica*, https://www.britannica.com/topic/Mesoamerican-civilization [accessed 19 June 2024].

Mursell, Ian 'The Use of Pulque in Aztec Culture', *Mexico Lore*, https://www.mexicolore.co.uk/aztecs/aztefacts/straw-poll [accessed 24 May 2024]

Chapter 4

Anderson, T., 'The Antiquity of T'ou Hu', *Asian Games Power*, https://sites.asiasociety.org/arts/asiangames/power01.html [accessed 23 September 2024]

Brown, Lynn, 'Wine in Ancient China', *Daily JSTOR*, https://daily.jstor.org/wine-in-ancient-china/ [accessed 5 September 2024]

Clart, Philip, 'The Concept of Ritual in the Thought of Sima Guang (1019–1086)', in *Perceptions of Antiquity in Chinese Civilization*, Dieter Kuhn and Helga Stahl (eds), (Heidelberg: Forum Verlag, 2008), https://home.uni-leipzig.de/clartp/Antiquity_Clart.pdf [accessed 20 September 2024]

'Arrow Holder', Cleveland Museum of Art, https://www.clevelandart.org/art/1957.65 [accessed 29 September 2024]

E-Wha, Lee, *Korea's Pastimes and Customs: A Social History*, trans. by Ju-Hee

Park (Paramus, NJ: Homa & Sekey Books, 2006), p. 83, https://books.google.co.uk/books?id=HcsMRc6pbQoC&pg=PA85&redir_esc=y#v=twopage&q&f=true [accessed 17 April 2024]

Loewe, Michael and Shaughnessy, Edward, 'Warring States: The Political History', *The Cambridge History of Ancient China*, summary, Cambridge University Press, https://www.cambridge.org/core/books/abs/cambridge-history-of-ancient-china/warring-states-political-history/1BCAF34A599BA322F3812203EB74F7D8 [accessed 17 April 2025]

McNair, Amy. *Xuanhe Catalogue of Paintings*, Chapter 13 (Ithaca: Cornell University Press, 2019), https://www.jstor.org/stable/10.7591/j.ctv310vjw1.21 [accessed 12 September 2024]

Montell, G., 'T'ou Hu: The Ancient Chinese Pitch-Pot Game', *Ethnos*, nos. 1–2: pp. 70–83 (1940), https://www.tandfonline.com/doi/abs/10.1080/00141844.1940.9980572 [accessed 21 September 2024]

Poo, Mu-Chou, 'The Use and Abuse of Wine in Ancient China', *Journal of the Economic and Social History of the Orient*, 42.2 (1999), pp. 123–51, https://www.jstor.org/stable/3632333 [accessed 17 September 2024]

Book of Rites (Liji), trans. by James Legge, *Chinese Notes*, https://chinesenotes.com/liji/liji040.html

Rudolph, Richard C., *The Antiquity of T'ou Hu*, https://sites.asiasociety.org/arts/asiangames/power01.html [accessed 5 September 2024]

Selby, Stephen, 'Chinese Archery', *Asian Traditional Archery Research Network*, http://www.atarn.org/training/chinese_archery_bckgrnd.htm [accessed 17 April 2025]

Chapter 5

Brepols Online, 'Food Culture in Poland', *Brepols Online*, https://www.brepolsonline.net/doi/pdf/10.1484/J.FOOD.1.100976 [accessed 17 April 2025].

Dynner, Glenn, *Yankel's Tavern: Jews, Liquor, and Life in the Kingdom of Poland* (New York: Oxford University Press, 2005)

Greenberg, Peter, 'The History of Vodka in Poland', *PeterGreenberg.com*, 15 October 2018, https://petergreenberg.com/2018/10/15/the-history-of-vodka-in-poland/ [accessed 17 April 2025]

Hodorowicz Knab, Sophie, *Polish Customs, Traditions, and Folklore*, foreword by Czesław Michał Krysa, illus. by Mary Anne Knab (New York: Hippocrene Books, 2003)

History of Poland, Encyclopaedia Britannica, https://www.britannica.com/place/Poland/History [accessed 17 April 2025]

If Not Vodka, Then What?, Culture.pl, https://culture.pl/en/article/if-not-vodka-then-what [accessed 17 April 2025]

Polish Customs, Traditions, and Folklore, Polish Culture NYC, https://www.polishculture-nyc.org/the-tradition-of-vodka-in-polish-culture/ [accessed 17 April 2025]

Poland's Double-Edged Vodka Tradition, MedicalXpress, 3 July 2018, https://medicalxpress.com/news/2018-07-poland-double-edged-vodka-tradition.html [accessed 17 April 2025]

'Polish Stereotypes and Vodka: How Communism Shaped National Identity', *Guardian*, 7 April 2011, https://www.theguardian.com/world/2011/apr/07/polish-sterotypes-vodka-communism [accessed 17 April 2025]

Thirst-Quenching Drinks from Poland's Past, Culture.pl, https://culture.pl/en/article/thirst-quenching-drinks-from-polands-past [accessed 17 April 2025]

Chapter 6

About, Edmond, *Rome of To-Day*, translated from the French (London: Hurst and Blackett, 1880). Available at: https://books.google.co.uk/books?id=2Go6AAAAMAAJ [accessed 20 September 2024]

Anonymous, *La Passatella: Spubbricate in Itajano e in Romanesco* (Rome: Edoardo Perino, 1889). Published anonymously; translated from Italian using machine translation. (Original in Italian). Available at: http://www.gruppodeiromanisti.it/wp-content/uploads/2014/10/1950.pdf [accessed 20 September 2024]

Cato, M. Porcius, *On Agriculture* (*De Agri Cultura*), trans. W. D. Hooper and H. B. Ash, Loeb Classical Library No. 283 (Cambridge, MA: Harvard University Press, 1934). Available at: https://www.loebclassics.com/view/LCL283/1934/pb_LCL283.xiii.xml [accessed 20 September 2024]

Darley, Gillian, 'Wonderful Things: The Experience of the Grand Tour', *Perspecta*, vol. 41, *Grand Tour* (2008), pp. 17–25, 28–9, published by The MIT Press on behalf of Perspecta. Available at: https://www.jstor.org/stable/40482307 [accessed 15 September 2024]

Davis, J., 'Passatella: An Economic Game', *The British Journal of Sociology*, vol. 15, no. 3 (September 1964), pp. 191–206, published by Wiley on behalf of the London School of Economics and Political Science. Available at: https://www.jstor.org/stable/588465 [accessed 3 August 2024]

Gruppo dei Romanisti, *Almanacco del Gruppo dei Romanisti, Anno XVII, 1950*. Available at: http://www.gruppodeiromanisti.it/wp-content/uploads/2014/10/1950.pdf [accessed 20 September 2024]

Haguenin, E., 'Un Poète Romain: Belli', *Revue des Deux Mondes* (1829–1971), CINQUIÈME PÉRIODE, vol. 8, no. 3 (April 1902), pp. 674–708. Available at: https://www.jstor.org/stable/44779165?seq=16 [accessed 20 September 2024]

Hom, Stephanie Malia, 'Consuming the View: Tourism, Rome, and the Topos of the Eternal City', *Annali d'Italianistica*, vol. 28, *Capital City: Rome 1870–2010* (2010), pp. 91–116, published by Arizona State University. Available at: https://www.jstor.org/stable/24016389 [accessed 18 September 2024]

Langworthy, Russell L., 'The Peasant World View: Italy and India', *Human Organization*, vol. 27, no. 3 (Fall 1968), pp. 212–19, published by the Society for Applied Anthropology. Available at: https://www.jstor.org/stable/44124580 [accessed 19 September 2024]

Nicassio, Susan Vandiver, *Imperial City: Rome under Napoleon* (Chicago: University of Chicago Press, 2005). Available at: https://dokumen.pub/imperial-city-rome-under-napoleon-9780226579740.html [accessed 20 September 2024]

Sturgis, Matthew, 'When in Rome – Oscar Wilde's Roman Sightseeing', *The Wildean*, no. 41 (July 2012), pp. 51–9, published by the Oscar Wilde Society. Available at: https://www.jstor.org/stable/45270314 [accessed 21 September 2024]

Thayer, William Roscoe, Review of *The Last Days of Papal Rome, 1850–1870* by R. De Cesare, Helen Zimmern, and G. M. Trevelyan, *The American Historical Review*, vol. 15, no. 2 (January 1910), pp. 388–9, published by Oxford University Press on behalf of the American Historical Association. Available at: https://www.jstor.org/stable/1838352 [accessed 21 September 2024]

Chapter 7

Bacon, Paul M., 'Art Patronage and Piety in Electoral Saxony: Frederick the Wise Promotes the Veneration of His Patron, St. Bartholomew', *The Sixteenth Century Journal*, vol. 39, no. 4 (Winter, 2008), pp. 973–1001

Bedini, Silvio A., 'The Role of Automata in the History of Technology', *Technology and Culture*, vol. 5, no. 1 (Winter, 1964), pp. 24–42. Available at: https://doi.org/10.2307/3101120 [accessed 20 September 2024]

Cantoni, Davide, 'Adopting a New Religion: The Case of Protestantism in 16th Century Germany', *The Economic Journal*, vol. 122, no. 560, Conference Papers (May 2012), pp. 502–531

Fliegel, Stephen N., 'The Cleveland Table Fountain and Gothic Automata', *Cleveland Studies in the History of Art*, vol. 7 (2002), pp. 6–49. Available at: https://www.jstor.org/stable/20079718 [accessed 20 September 2024]

Friess, Joachim, *Diana and the Stag*, circa 1620, silver, German, Augsburg. The Metropolitan Museum of Art, New York, Accession Number 17.190.746. Available at: https://www.metmuseum.org/art/collection/search/193623 [accessed 26 September 2024]

Hendrix, Scott H., 'Loyalty, Piety, or Opportunism: German Princes and the Reformation', *Journal of Interdisciplinary History*, vol. XXV, no. 2 (Autumn 1994), pp. 211–24

'Huntsman Automaton', The British Museum, WB.134, 1617–20, silver-gilt automaton figure, *Curatorial Notes:* Text from Tait 1988. London. Available at: https://wb.britishmuseum.org/MCN2560#1500443001 [accessed 20 September 2024]

King, Rachel, 'The Automaton that is also a Drinking Game', with Rachel King, Curator's Corner S7 Ep9', *YouTube, The British Museum YouTube Channel.* Available at: https://www.youtube.com/watch?v=VXjp64dnw4s#:~: text= The%20 Automaton%20that%20is%20also%20a%20Drinking,%7C%20 Curator%27s%20Corner%20S7%20Ep9%20%2D%20YouTube [accessed 20 September 2024]

Martyris, Nina, 'The Other Reformation: How Martin Luther Changed Our Beer, Too', *NPR Illinois*, 31 October 2017. Available at: https://www.nprillinois.org/health-harvest/2017-10-31/the-other-reformation-how-martin-luther-changed-our-beer-too [accessed 18 April 2025]

Moran, Bruce T., 'Princes, Machines and the Valuation of Precision in the 16th Century', *Sudhoffs Archiv*, Bd. 61, H. 3 (1977 3. Quartal), pp. 209–228

Price, Derek J. de Solla, 'Automata and the Origins of Mechanism and Mechanistic Philosophy', *Technology and Culture*, vol. 5, no. 1 (Winter, 1964), pp. 9–23. Available at: https://www.jstor.org/stable/3101119 [accessed 20 September 2024]

Chapter 8

Anna Sorokina, 'Russian Moonshine: What is Samogon?', *Russia Beyond*, 23 October 2019 https://www.rbth.com/russian-kitchen/331175-russian-moonshine-samogon [accessed 24 October 2024]

BBC News, 'Churchill and Stalin Made "Merry" Until Early Hours, (23 May 2013), https://www.bbc.co.uk/news/uk-22623251 [accessed 25 October 2024]

Bhattacharya, J., Gathmann, C. and Miller, G., 'The Gorbachev Anti-Alcohol Campaign and Russia's Mortality Crisis', *American Economic Journal: Applied Economics*, 5.2 (2013), pp. 232–260, https://www.jstor.org/stable/43189436 [accessed 3 October 2024]

British Medical Journal, 'The Russian Vodka Monopoly', 2.2855 (1915), pp. 444–5, https://www.jstor.org/stable/25314797 [accessed 8 October 2024]

Brown, H., 'Drinking Games: Can Russia Admit It Has a Problem?', *World Policy Journal*, 28.2 (2011), pp. 111–21, https://www.jstor.org/stable/41479388 [accessed 6 October 2024]

Christian, D., 'Vodka and Corruption in Russia on the Eve of Emancipation', *Slavic Review*, 46.3 (1987), pp. 471–88, https://www.jstor.org/stable/2498098 [accessed 8 October 2024]

Connor, W. D., 'Alcohol and Soviet Society', *Slavic Review*, 30.3 (1971), pp. 570–88, https://www.jstor.org/stable/2493544 [accessed 9 October 2024]

Corbesero, S., 'History, Myth, and Memory: A Biography of a Stalin Portrait', *Russian History*, 38.1 (2011), pp. 58–84, https://www.jstor.org/stable/24665382 [accessed 10 October 2024]

Daly, J., review of *Vodka Politics: Alcohol, Autocracy, and the Secret History of the Russian State*, by Mark Lawrence Schrad, *The American Historical Review*, 120.1 (2015), p. 359, https://www.jstor.org/stable/10.1093/ahr/120.1.359 [accessed 11 October 2024]

Dursteler, E. R., 'Bad Bread and the "Outrageous Drunkenness of the Turks": Food and Identity in the Accounts of Early Modern European

Travelers to the Ottoman Empire', *Journal of World History*, 25.2/3 (2014), pp. 203–28, https://www.jstor.org/stable/43818480 [accessed 12 October 2024]

Hall, Chris, 'Getting Pickled with Joseph Stalin', *JSTOR Daily*, 10 January 2024, https://daily.jstor.org/getting-pickled-with-joseph-stalin/ [accessed 22 October 2024]

Herlihy, P., 'Joy of the Rus': Rites and Rituals of Russian Drinking', *The Russian Review*, 50.2 (1991), pp. 131–47, https://www.jstor.org/stable/131155 [accessed 8 October 2024]

Herrold, M., 'Which Truth? Cultural Politics and Vodka in Rural Russia', *Geographical Review*, 91.1/2 (2001), pp. 295–303, https://www.jstor.org/stable/3250830 [accessed 13 October 2024]

Hivon, M., 'Vodka: The "Spirit" of Exchange', *The Cambridge Journal of Anthropology*, 17.3 (1994), pp. 1–18, https://www.jstor.org/stable/23818683 [accessed 14 October 2024]

Jordan, John M., 'A Small World of Little Americans: The $1 Diplomacy of Wendell Willkie's *One World*', *Indiana Magazine of History*, 88.3 (September 1992), pp. 173–204

Mäkinen, I. H. and Reitan, T. C., 'Continuity and Change in Russian Alcohol Consumption from the Tsars to Transition', *Social History*, 31.2 (2006), pp. 160–79, https://www.jstor.org/stable/4287330 [accessed 15 October 2024]

Morrissey, S. K., 'Drinking to Death: Suicide, Vodka and Religious Burial in Russia', *Past & Present*, 186 (2005), pp. 117–146, https://www.jstor.org/stable/3600853 [accessed 16 October 2024]

Office for Budget Responsibility, *Alcohol Duties*, October 2024, https://obr.uk/forecasts-in-depth/tax-by-tax-spend-by-spend/alcohol-duties/ [accessed 24 November 2024]

Pokhlebkin, V. V., Renfrey Clarke (trans) *History of Vodka*, (Verso, 1992)

Politico, Schrad, M. L., 'The Vodka Effect: Happy New Year – A Short History of Booze Diplomacy', *Politico Magazine*, 30 December 2013, https://www.politico.com/magazine/story/2013/12/vodka-russia-foreign-policy-101613/ [accessed 17 October 2024]

Pridemore, William Alex, 'Heavy Drinking and Suicide in Russia', *Social Forces*, 85.1 (September 2006), pp. 413–430 https://www.jstor.org/stable/3844421 [accessed 24 October 2024]

Schrad, M. L., *Vodka Politics: Alcohol, Autocracy, and the Secret History of the Russian State*, reviewed by J. Daly, *The American Historical Review*, 120.1 (2015), p. 359. https://www.jstor.org/stable/10.1093/ahr/120.1.359 [accessed 11 October 2024]

Shlapentokh, D., 'Drunkenness and Anarchy in Russia: A Case of Political Culture', *Russian History*, 18.4 (1991), pp. 457–500, https://www.jstor.org/stable/24656607 [accessed 18 October 2024]

Stakhov, D. and Newlin, T., 'The Prose (and Cons) of Vodka', *Gastronomica*, 5.1 (2005), pp. 25–8, https://www.jstor.org/stable/10.1525/gfc.2005.5.1.25 [accessed 19 October 2024]

Tekin, E., 'Employment, Wages, and Alcohol Consumption in Russia', *Southern Economic Journal*, 71.2 (2004), pp. 397–417, https://www.jstor.org/stable/4135298 [accessed 20 October 2024]

Treml, V. G., 'Death from Alcohol Poisoning in the USSR', *Soviet Studies*, 34.4 (1982), pp. 487–505, https://www.jstor.org/stable/151904 [accessed 8 October 2024]

Walker, S., 'Can Russia Start a Drinking Revolution?', *British Medical Journal*, 343.7820 (2011), pp. 396–8, https://www.jstor.org/stable/23051108 [accessed 21 October 2024]

Web Article, *L'histoire de la Vodka, Caviar Passion,* https://www.caviarpassion.com/en/content/78-l-histoire-de-la-vodka.html [accessed 23 October 2024]

Chapter 9

Bavipower.com, *Viking Drinking Tradition*, Available at: https://bavipower.com/blogs/bavipower-viking-blog/viking-drinking-tradition [accessed January 2025]

Bivrost, *Drinking Customs of the Vikings*, Available at: https://www.bivrost.com/drinking-customs-of-the-vikings/ [Accessed January 2025]

Cunliffe, B., *Facing the Ocean: The Atlantic and Its Peoples 8000 BC–AD 1500* (Oxford, 2001), p. 494

Gardeła, L., 'What the Vikings Did for Fun? Sports and Pastimes in Medieval Northern Europe', *World Archaeology*, vol. 44, no. 2 (June 2012), pp. 234–47. Published by: Taylor & Francis, Ltd. Available at: https://www.jstor.org/stable/23210597 [accessed January 2025]

Guerrero Rodriguez, J. F., *Old Norse Drinking Culture* (PhD thesis, University of Leeds, 2015), p. 191. Available at: https://etheses.whiterose.ac.uk/14217/1/542807.pdf [accessed January 2025]

Lyme Bay Winery, *The Truth Behind Vikings and Mead*. Available at: https://lymebaywinery.co.uk/blog/the-truth-behind-vikings-and-mead/?srslti d=AfmBOopIuanpZLKJpu5BTssp5T1qfiU41mi7V0yfDxOYnpl9Oz3 ORY2t [accessed January 2025]

Norse Spirit, *The Different Types of Drinking Vessels in Viking Culture*. Available at: https://norsespirit.com/blogs/norse_viking_blog/the-different-types-of-drinking-vessels-in-viking-culture?srsltid=AfmBOopoUqi0w6Z5cHQvR9jNyfABVfprYgPByu5NaZ4MD3vmWJu5jkra [accessed January 2025]

Riseley, C., *Ceremonial Drinking in the Viking Age* (Masteroppgave i Viking and Medieval Norse Studies, Det humanistiske fakultetet, Institutt for lingvistiske og nordiske studier, Våren 2014)

Rood, J., *Drinking With Óðinn: Alcohol and Religion in Heathen Scandinavia* (Reykjavík, 2014), p. 7. Available at: https://www.academia.edu/8640034/Drinking_with_%C3%93%C3%B0inn_Alcohol_and_Religion_in_Heathen_Scandinavia [accessed January 2025]

Skjalden.com, *Viking Mead*. Available at: https://skjalden.com/viking-mead/ [accessed January 2025]

Chapter 10

Binswanger, J., 'Ancient Egyptians Drank Psychedelic Concoctions from 2000-Year-Old Mug, Study Finds', *Smithsonian Magazine – Smart News*, 25 November 2024. Available at: https://www.smithsonianmag.com/smart-news/ancient-egyptians-drank-psychedelic-concoctions-from-this-2000-year-old-mug-study-finds-180985500/ [accessed January 2025]

El-Gawhary, K., 'Religious Fermentation', *MERIP*, Summer 1999, no. 211. Available at: https://merip.org/1999/06/religious-fermentation/ [accessed January 2025]

Emboden, W. A., 'The Sacred Narcotic Lily of the Nile: Nymphaea caerulea', *Economic Botany*, vol. 32, no. 4 (Oct.–Dec. 1978), pp. 395–407. Published by: Springer on behalf of New York Botanical Garden Press. Available at: https://www.jstor.org/stable/4253981 [accessed January 2025]

Fletcher, J., 'Wine in Ancient Egypt I', *Immortal Egypt* blog, 24 Jan. 2024. Available at: https://www.immortalegypt.co.uk/post/wine-in-ancient-egypt-i [Accessed January 2025]

Fletcher, J., 'Wine in Ancient Egypt II', *Immortal Egypt* blog, 27 Feb. 2024. Available at: https://www.immortalegypt.co.uk/post/wine-in-ancient-egypt-ii [accessed January 2025]

Garstang Museum Admin, 'Hathor: The Goddess to Get a Beer or Glass of Milk With', *Garstang Museum Blog*, 5 Aug. 2020. Available at: https://

garstangmuseum.wordpress.com/2020/08/05/hathor-the-goddess-to-get-a-beer-or-glass-of-milk-with/ [accessed January 2025]

Hubbell, D., 'Ancient Egyptians' Cocktails', *Atlas Obscura*, 26 Feb. 2024. Available at: https://www.atlasobscura.com/articles/ancient-egyptians-cocktails [accessed January 2025]

Homan, M. M., 'Beer and Its Drinkers: An Ancient Near Eastern Love Story', *Near Eastern Archaeology*, vol. 67, no. 2 (Jun. 2004), pp. 84–95. Published by: The University of Chicago Press on behalf of The American Schools of Oriental Research. Available at: https://www.jstor.org/stable/4132364 [accessed January 2025]

Homan, M. M., 'Beer Production by Throwing Bread into Water: A New Interpretation of Qoh. XI 1–2', *Vetus Testamentum*, vl. 52, fasc. 2 (Apr. 2002), pp. 275–8. Published by: Brill. Available at: https://www.jstor.org/stable/1585093 [accessed January 2025]

Homebrewers Association, *Pharaoh Ale: Brewing a Replica of an Ancient Egyptian Beer*. Available at: www.homebrewersassociation.org/zymurgy/pharaoh-ale-brewing-a-replica-of-an-ancient-egyptian-beer/ [accessed January 2025]

Jennings, J., Antrobus, K. L., Atencio, S. J., Glavich, E., Johnson, R., Loffler, G. and Luu, C., '"Drinking Beer in a Blissful Mood": Alcohol Production, Operational Chains, and Feasting in the Ancient World', *Current Anthropology*, vol. 46, no. 2 (Apr. 2005), pp. 275–303. Published by: The University of Chicago Press on behalf of Wenner-Gren Foundation for Anthropological Research. Available at: https://www.jstor.org/stable/10.1086/427119 [accessed January 2025]

King, A., 'Food & Drink in Ancient Egypt', *World History Encyclopedia*, 9 July 2024. Available at: https://www.worldhistory.org/article/2494/food--drink-in-ancient-egypt/ [accessed January 2025]

Marks, T., 'Sip of History: Ancient Egyptian Beer', *British Museum Blog*, 25 May 2018. Available at: https://www.britishmuseum.org/blog/sip-history-ancient-egyptian-beer [accessed January 2025]

McGovern, P. E., Mirzoian, A., Hall, G. R. and Bar-Yosef, O., 'Ancient Egyptian Herbal Wines', *Proceedings of the National Academy of Sciences of the United States of America*, vol. 106, no. 18 (5 May 2009), pp. 7361–6. Published by: National Academy of Sciences. Available at: https://www.jstor.org/stable/40483278 [accessed January 2025]

McGovern, P. E., 'Wine of Egypt's Golden Age: An Archaeochemical Perspective', *The Journal of Egyptian Archaeology*, vol. 83 (1997), pp. 69–108. Published by: Sage Publications, Ltd. Available at: https://www.jstor.org/stable/3822459 [accessed January 2025]

Merola, M., 'Letters to the Crocodile God', *Archaeology*, vol. 60, no. 6 (Nov./Dec. 2007), pp. 22–7. Published by: Archaeological Institute of America. Available at: https://www.jstor.org/stable/41780302 [accessed January 2025]

Mojsov, B., 'The Ancient Egyptian Underworld in the Tomb of Sety I: Sacred Books of Eternal Life', *The Massachusetts Review*, vol. 42, no. 4 (Winter 2001/2002), pp. 489–506. Published by: The Massachusetts Review, Inc. Available at: https://www.jstor.org/stable/25091798 [accessed January 2025]

Plutarch, 'Inimitable Livers', in *Perseus Digital Library*. Available at: https://www.perseus.tufts.edu/hopper/searchresults?q=inimitable+livers [accessed January 2025]

Rhakotis, 'Sobek: Ancient Egyptian Crocodile God in the Greek and Roman Periods'. Available at: https://rhakotis.com/2018/01/30/sobek-ancient-egyptian-crocodile-god-in-the-greek-and-roman-periods/ [accessed January 2025]

Spalinger, A. J., 'Eleventh Day, Twelfth Night: Further Remarks Concerning Three Feasts in Egyptian Civil Thoth', *Studien zur Altägyptischen Kultur*, Bd. 43 (2014), pp. 399–415. Published by: Helmut Buske Verlag GmbH. Available at: https://www.jstor.org/stable/44160283 [accessed January 2025]

Ullman, B. L., 'Cleopatra's Pearls', *The Classical Journal*, vol. 52, no. 5 (2025). Available at: https://penelope.uchicago.edu/Thayer/E/Journals/CJ/52/5/Cleopatras_Pearls*.html [accessed January 2025].

Williams, S., 'Ancient Raving: Egyptian Festival of Drunkenness', *Business Trends Around the Globe Blog*, [No publication date]. Available at: http://heritage-key.com/blogs/sean-williams/ancient-raving-egyptian-festival-drunkenness/ [accessed January 2025]

Chapter 11

Barr, A., *Drink: A Social History of America* (New York: Carroll & Graf Publishers, 1999)

BBC News, 'The Surprising British Origins of the US National Anthem', BBC, 15 April 2024. Available at: https://www.bbc.co.uk/news/articles/cp4w2g1pq5go [accessed January 2025]

Behr, E., *Prohibition: The 13 Years That Changed America* (New York: Arcade Publishing, 1997)

Burns, E., *The Spirits of America: A Social History of Alcohol* (Philadelphia: Temple University Press, 2004)

Erenberg, L. A., 'From New York to Middletown: Repeal and the Legitimization of Nightlife in the Great Depression', *American Quarterly*, vol. 38, no. 5 (Winter, 1986), pp. 761–78. Available at: https://doi.org/10.2307/2712822 [accessed February 2025]

Grasse, S., *Colonial Spirits: A Toast to Our Drunken History* (New York: Abrams Image, 2016)

Lupton, M. J., 'Ladies' Entrance: Women and Bars', *Feminist Studies*, vol. 5, no. 3 (Autumn, 1979), pp. 571–88. Available at: https://doi.org/10.2307/3177514 [accessed February 2025]

National Park Service, *Tobacco: Colonial Cultivation Methods*, NPS.gov. Available at: https://www.nps.gov/jame/learn/historyculture/tobacco-colonial-cultivation-methods.htm [accessed January 2025]

Rorabaugh, W. J., *Prohibition: A Very Short Introduction* (Oxford: Oxford University Press, 2020). Available at: https://doi.org/10.1093/actrade/9780199739981.001.0001 [accessed February 2025]

Chapter 12

Burns, Robert,. 'Tam O' Shanter', in *Complete Works of Robert Burns*. Available at: http://www.robertburns.org.uk/Assets/Poems_Songs/tamoshanter.htm [accessed February 2025]

Cook, Anthony. *A History of Drinking: The Scottish Pub Since 1700* (Edinburgh: Edinburgh University Press, 2015). Available at: https://www.euppublishing.com/userimages/ContentEditor/1439825554690/A%20History%20of%20Drinking%20Sample.pdf [accessed February 2025]

Dietz, Vivien E., 'The Politics of Whisky: Scottish Distillers, the Excise, and the Pittite State', *Journal of British Studies*, 36.1 (January 1997), pp. 35–69. Available at: https://www.jstor.org/stable/175902 [accessed February 2025]

Hames, G. *Alcohol in World History* (London: Routledge, 2012)

Holt (ed.), *A Social and Cultural History of Alcohol* (Oxford: Berg, 2006)

Knox, W. W., 'The Attack of the "Half-Formed Persons": the 1811–2 Tron Riot in Edinburgh Revisited', *The Scottish Historical Review*, 91.232, Part 2 (October 2012), pp. 287–310. Available at: https://www.jstor.org/stable/43773919 [accessed February 2025]

Ludington, Charles C., '"To the King O'er the Water": Scotland and Claret c. 1660–1763', in Holt (ed.) *A Social and Cultural History of Alcohol* (Oxford: Berg, 2006)

Merriam-Webster. 'High Jinks – Meaning and Origin', *Merriam-Webster Dictionary*. Available at: https://www.merriam-webster.com/wordplay/high-jinks-meaning-origin [accessed February 2025]

Phrases.org.uk. 'High Jinks', *The Phrase Finder*. Available at: https://www.phrases.org.uk/meanings/high-jinks.html [accessed February 2025]

Quiet Writer, The, 'Friars Carse, Robert Burns and a Drinking Contest', *The Quiet Writer*, 6 April 2018. Available at: https://thequietwriter.com/2018/04/06/friars-carse-robert-burns-and-a-drinking-contest-atozchallenge/ [accessed February 2025]

Scotch Whisky Association. 'Story of Scotch', Scotch-Whisky.org. Available at: https://www.scotch-whisky.org.uk/discover-scotch/story-of-scotch/ [accessed February 2025]

Scott, Walter, *Guy Mannering* (1815). Available at: http://public-library.uk/ebooks/42/96.pdf [accessed February 2025]

Way With Words, 'High Jinks: Origin and Meaning', WayWordRadio.org, https://waywordradio.org/high-jinks-origin-and-meaning/ [accessed February 2025]

Chapter 13

Akyeampong, Emmanuel Kwaku, *Drink, Power, and Cultural Change: A Social History of Alcohol in Ghana, c. 1800 to Recent Times* (Oxford: Currey, 1996)

Ambler, Charles, 'Alcohol in Africa', *Oxford Bibliographies*, https://www.oxfordbibliographies.com/display/document/obo-9780199846733/obo-9780199846733-0220.xml [accessed March 2025]

Boston University, 'Alcohol and Disorder in Precolonial Africa', ASC Working Papers in African Studies Series, 1987, https://hdl.handle.net/2144/41081 [accessed March 2025]

Encyclopaedia Britannica, 'Ghana: History', *Britannica*, https://www.britannica.com/place/Ghana [accessed March 2025]

Pan, Lynn, *Alcohol in Colonial Africa* (Helsinki: Finnish Foundation for Alcohol Studies; New Brunswick, NJ: Rutgers University Center of Alcohol Studies, 1975)

Chapter 14

Durrani, Nadia, 'Oldest Wine from Jiahu, China', *World Archaeology*. https://www.world-archaeology.com/world/asia/china/oldest-wine-from-jiahu-china

Edwards, E. D. and Li Shang-yin, 'The Miscellanea of I-shan: A Little-Known Work of Li Shang-yin', *Bulletin of the School of Oriental Studies*, University of London, vol. 5, no. 4, 1930, pp. 757–85. Published by Cambridge University Press on behalf of the School of Oriental and African Studies. https://www.jstor.org/stable/607017

Ferrara, Mark S., 'Patterns of Fate in "Dream of the Red Chamber"', *Interdisciplinary Literary Studies*, vol. 11, no. 1, Fall 2009, pp. 12–31. Published by Penn State University Press. https://www.jstor.org/stable/41210028

Froissart, Pauline, and Dan Martin, 'Tough Sell: Baijiu, China's Potent Tipple, Looks Abroad', *The Jakarta Post*, 18 June 2019. Originally published by Agence France-Presse. https://www.thejakartapost.com/life/2019/06/17/tough-sell-baijiu-chinas-potent-tipple-looks-abroad.html

Guo, Jie, 'Games in Late Ming and Early Qing Erotic Literature' in *Games and Play in Chinese and Sinophone Cultures*, Li Guo, Douglas Eyman and Hongmei Sun (eds), pp. 100–116 (Seattle: University of Washington Press, 2024). http://www.jstor.org/stable/jj.23996201.10. [accessed 18 April 2025]

Guo, Li, 'The Courtesans' Drinking Games in "The Dream in the Green Bower"', in *Games and Play in Chinese and Sinophone Cultures*, Li Guo, Douglas Eyman and Hongmei Sun (eds), pp. 117–37 (Seattle: University of Washington Press, 2024). http://www.jstor.org/stable/jj.23996201.11. [accessed 18 April 2025]

Lo, Andrew, 'The Game of Leaves: An Inquiry into the Origin of Chinese Playing Cards', *Bulletin of the School of Oriental and African Studies*, University of London, vol. 63, no. 3, 2000, pp. 389–406. Published by Cambridge University Press on behalf of the School of Oriental and African Studies. https://www.jstor.org/stable/1559494

Louis, François, 'The Hejiacun Rhyton and the Chinese Wine Horn (gong): Intoxicating Rarities and Their Antiquarian History', *Artibus Asiae*, vol. 67, no. 2, 2007, pp. 201–242. Published by Artibus Asiae Publishers. https://www.jstor.org/stable/25261880

Lu, Rong, 'Family and Gender' in *A Ming Confucian's World: Selections from Miscellaneous Records from the Bean Garden* (Seattle: University of Washington Press, 2022). https://www.jstor.org/stable/j.ctv2n4w5w9.9

Poo, Mu-Chou, 'The Use and Abuse of Wine in Ancient China', *Journal of the Economic and Social History of the Orient*, vol. 42, no. 2, 1999, pp. 123–51. Published by Brill. https://www.jstor.org/stable/3632333

Rudolph, Richard C., 'Notes on the Riddle in China', *California Folklore Quarterly*, vol. 1, no. 1, Jan. 1942, pp. 65–82. Published by Western States Folklore Society. https://www.jstor.org/stable/1495728

Saarela, Mårten Söderblom, '"Shooting Characters": A Phonological Game and Its Uses in Late Imperial China', *Journal of the American Oriental Society*, vol. 138, no. 2, Apr.–June 2018, pp. 327–59. Published by American Oriental Society. https://www.jstor.org/stable/10.7817/jameroriesoci.138.2.0327

Unknown author, *The Story of Baijiu*. Drink Baijiu. https://drinkbaijiu.com/bai-ology/the-story-of-baijiu/

Unknown author, *Chinese Wine Culture*, *ChinaCulture.org*. http://en.chinaculture.org/library/2008-01/08/content_127188.htm

Yao Wan and Thawascha Dechsubha, 'A Survey of Traditional Chinese Drinking Games', *Technium Social Sciences Journal*, vol. 31, no. 1, 2022, pp. 728–41. www.researchgate.net/publication/360488795_A_Survey_of_Traditional_Chinese_Drinking_Games